ADVENTURE IN COOKING

DUCKS UNLIMITED

POULTRY ▪ MEATS ▪ FISH & FINISHING TOUCHES

TABLE OF CONTENTS

BIRDS

We have used farmed game birds for our recipes, but wild can be substituted and the various types can be interchanged. Remember that ducks and geese (domestic) are very fatty and their skin needs to be pricked before cooking. Duck and geese breasts should ideally be cooked rare. On the other hand, partridges, quail, Cornish game hens and pheasant are more similar to chicken and turkey in terms of behaviour in cooking. Grouse is a category on its own! Chicken and turkey are good substitutions for any of the recipes in this section.

GAME

A variety of different types of game or meat can be used in most of our recipes. Because most of the game available to us in supermarkets is farmed, the flavours are constant and predictable and the tenderness is assured. With some exceptions (rabbit for example), game should be cooked rare or medium rare and sliced as thinly as possible. If you are fortunate enough to have a hunter in the family, remember that wild game is not as tender and needs longer, slower cooking or "larding" (added fat). Try two of the newest meats on the market in some of our recipes – muskox and ostrich (strictly speaking a bird but cooked and served like a meat).

FISH

We have shown these recipes in a variety of fish species but substitution is possible in nearly every recipe. For substitution purposes, the species fall roughly into 4 categories: shellfish (mussels, clams, prawns, crab, shrimp, scallops), white fish (orange roughy, sole, cod, snapper, halibut), salmons (salmon, Arctic char, trout) and "meat-like"fish (swordfish, tuna, shark). Remember that nearly all fish and shellfish are better slightly under-cooked rather than over-cooked. High heat and approximately 10 minutes per 1" (2.5 cm) of thickness is a good rule of thumb.

FINISHING TOUCHES

In this chapter we have given you a selection of recipes to complete your meal after choosing from the previous 3 chapters for your main course. Several could easily be turned into main course meals by the addition of game, birds or fish. For example, rare ostrich slices added to the Chèvre Stacks on page 73 would be delicious; cold duck would fit beautifully in the Bulgar Salad on page 76; scallops or prawns could easily be added to the Penne with Sun-Dried Tomato Cream on page 74 and fresh poached salmon chunks would go well in the Gnocchi with Pesto Sauce on page 76.

DUCKS UNLIMITED

NOAH'S ARK ON THE CANADIAN PRAIRIES

Why would a group of American sportsmen in the middle of the Great Depression form an organization to save wetlands on the Canadian prairies? Because they knew that these were the breeding grounds for 70 percent of North America's waterfowl. In the dust and drought of the 1930s, wetlands were disappearing. Marshlands turned bone dry after broods were hatched. Nesting havens became death traps. Once, there had been 400 million ducks on this continent, nearly half nesting in Canada's prairie provinces – Alberta, Saskatchewan, Manitoba. By 1934, waterfowl population had dropped to 27 million.

The organization these men created rose phoenix-like from the grasshopper plagued Dirty Thirties to become North America's greatest conservation movement: Ducks Unlimited. Between 1938 and 1997, Ducks Unlimited mounted more than 15,000 projects across Canada, the United States and Mexico, preserving and creating habitat for more than 600 species of wildlife – birds, mammals, fish, amphibians, reptiles and plants, including 160 endangered species. Creatures from the calliope hummingbird to the Tennessee warbler, the pronghorn antelope to the Pacific jumping mouse, have had their survival protected by Ducks Unlimited. DU has become a kind of wetlands/uplands Noah's Ark.

At the helm at the beginning was Joseph P. Knapp, a powerful publisher and sportsman who had supported Dwight Huntington's Game Conservation Institute in New Jersey. In 1930, Knapp and friends, including financier J. Pierpont Morgan and cartoonist "Ding" Darling, established a foundation called More Game Birds in America. Knapp's group outlined a ten-year program for protection of game birds, publishing the data they gathered in "More Waterfowl by Assisting Nature." Among their recommendations: creation of an international agency to increase waterfowl population, restoration of breeding grounds, control of water levels, food and coverage provision, control of natural enemies, fire prevention, a halt to unauthorized grazing, suppression of shooting on breeding grounds, and development of refuges along migration routes. President Franklin D. Roosevelt's Committee on Wildlife Restoration was established in 1934, in response to a memorandum from More Game Birds in America.

In 1935, the foundation conducted the first International Wild Bird Census, ranging from the potholes of the prairies to the glacial lakes of the Northwest Territories. The survey indicated that growth and survival of the duck population demanded conservation of Canadian breeding grounds. Knapp and his friends determined they would "drought-proof the prairies."

Joe Knapp and some of the More Game Birds group were at Knapp's fishing camp on Beaverkill River in New York State's Catskill Mountains when Game Conservation Institute director Arthur Bartley, who had made annual trips to Canada during

the waterfowl breeding season since 1929, suggested a new organization to be called Ducks Limited. "Damn it," snapped Knapp, "we don't want limited ducks." "All right, then," countered Bartley, "make it Ducks Unlimited." Ducks Unlimited, Inc. was incorporated in the United States January 29, 1937. Ducks Unlimited Canada was created that same year, on March 10. Bartley was named senior executive officer.

DUCK FACTORY NUMBER ONE

Bartley's first move was to establish three waterfowl habitat restoration projects, one in each prairie province. Big Grass Marsh west of Lake Manitoba, 40,000 acres (16,000 hectares) ravaged by dust storms and peat fires, was Duck Factory Number One. Saskatchewan's site was Waterhen Marsh, 65 miles (104 kilometres) southeast of Prince Albert, at the headwaters of the Carrot River, drained for farmland in the 1920s and later swept by peat fires. In Alberta, the new conservators chose Many Island Lake, 8,000 wetland acres (3,200 hectares) which had been a federal bird sanctuary in the 1920s. By 1935, the only water it held to sustain thousands of birds was in puddles left by hoofprints.

THE MAIN MEN

Drafted to direct these projects was 52-year old Thomas C. Main, a surface water engineer for Canadian National Railways recently returned from Bermuda, where he had been loaned to consult on engineering and water supply. Born in England, raised in Pincher Creek, Alberta, Tom Main was a long-chinned man with an explosion of snowy hair, a wide grin, and a right eye almost closed, as the result of an injury. Some said he had been hit in the eye by a falling mallard. Main never denied it.

Main, said wildlife artist Angus Shortt, was "on fire with mission." As general manager for Ducks Unlimited Canada, he quickly brought on board Ed Russenholt, then public relations manager for the Wawanesa Insurance Company, as his assistant. "Come on home," Main wrote, "we've got the chance to do the job we've always wanted to do." Russenholt assembled a force of 3,200 prairie volunteers, called Kee-Men, to carry out another waterfowl census in 1938. "We did whatever we could to help Ducks Unlimited," said rancher George Scott.

Appointed chief naturalist was Bertram W. Cartwright, a founding member of the Manitoba Natural History Society, writer of the Winnipeg Tribune column "Wild Things," and an authority on bird calls. "One of the things co-workers remember most vividly about Bert Cartwright," wrote Ducks Unlimited chief biologist William G. Leitch in "Ducks and Men," "was his ability to fly on aerial surveys through the roughest air without apparent discomfort." An aerial survey from Winnipeg to Great

Slave Lake in 1938 took 49 hours and 45 minutes, in a single-engine, high-wing, pontooned monoplane. "While men were going through the agonies of air sickness," wrote Leitch, a World War Two RCAF squadron leader, "Bert bounced happily up and down, recording ducks, geese, pelicans and anything else that interested him."*

Ducks Unlimited projects showed rapid results. US backers had raised $100,000 for the first year's operations, hoping to restore 100,000 acres (40,000 hectares) of waterfowl breeding grounds, but, by the end of 1938, 155,000 acres (62,000 hectares) had been restored. In 1939,the duck population on prairie wetlands was just under 60 million, 21.7 percent higher than in 1938 and 47.4 percent higher than in 1935. By 1947, prairie waterfowl population had reached 110 million.

The pelican is regarded as a tropical bird, but white pelicans nest from Primrose Lake, Saskatchewan, to Great Salt Lake, Utah, and brown pelicans are at home across the southern US to the Pacific coast.

FAST FORWARD

By 1997, the international Ducks Unlimited group included the Canadian and US bodies, Ducks Unlimited de Mexico (DUMAC) and Ducks Unlimited New Zealand Incorporated, operating in New Zealand and Australia. The organization was active from Yukon to Yucatan, with projects from 10-acre (four-hectare) potholes to river deltas stretching over 1.25 million acres (500,000 hectares).

Ducks Unlimited expertise was also at work in other countries, Egypt to Brazil. The organization's Canadian headquarters, Oak Hammock Marsh Interpretive Centre, outside Winnipeg, Manitoba, led a workshop in the Bahamas, focusing on wetland loss and the decline of the West Indian whistling duck. Ron Coley, chief engineer for Ducks Unlimited (Canada), traveled between Africa and eastern Europe's Commonwealth of Independent States (the former USSR). In Botswana, location of Africa's largest oasis, Coley showed villagers how to save wetlands, end poaching, and enjoy greater economic success through the development of ventures like safari camps. In Uzbekistan, where wetlands had suffered a half-century of neglect, he demonstrated how to begin programs of reclamation. In Ukraine, he introduced soft-mouthed hunting dogs to retrieve game birds, helping hunters to bag their limit without over-shooting.

"HELLO, I'M GEORGE BUSH

AND YOUR CALL IS IMPORTANT TO ME."

Callers to Ducks Unlimited's US headquarters in Memphis,

Tennessee, may be surprised to hear a familiar voice on the line: "This is President George Bush. Join Ducks Unlimited today for a better tomorrow."

George Bush is a card-carrying Ducks Unlimited member. So are President Bill Clinton and Vice President Al Gore. The organization has more than a million supporters across North America, including Morgan Freeman, who also turns up on the Memphis answering machine. Other spokespersons over the years have included John Wayne, Bing Crosby, Cliff Robertson, Walter Payton and Ted Turner, whose network carries the Ducks Unlimited TV program-"The World of Ducks Unlimited."

There are also thousands of volunteers involved. Some have logged more than 3,000 hours of volunteer activity. "Their passion," said one Ducks Unlimited program organizer, "is so strong for what we do. They know it affects not just wildlife; it affects everybody."

GREENWINGS FOR THE FUTURE

Education of youngsters is a priority for Ducks Unlimited. More than 10,000 children are members of its Greenwing program. Busloads of students are taken on tours to conservation centres outside Winnipeg and Fredericton, New Brunswick. Across Canada, students take part in Greenwing wetland quest field days. Others learn about Greenwing through the Wetland Wizard

Adventure comic book; "Puddler", a magazine and "Marshworld" an illustrated guide to wetlands, both published by Ducks Unlimited in Memphis. Greenwing has produced guides for volunteers and resources for classroom use by teachers, and has established schoolyard habitat projects. "This is essential," said one Ducks Unlimited director. "These youngsters are the landowners, conservationists, taxpayers, voters and politicians of the future."

From a log cabin on Big Grass Marsh in 1938, Ducks Unlimited Canada has grown to a coast-to-coast network (Fullerton Marsh, Prince Edward Island, to Reiswig Slough, British Columbia) of more than 40 field offices with a staff of 500 and an annual budget of $55 million, 87 percent of which goes to habitat protection. In the US, Ducks Unlimited is active in all 50 states. Internationally, the organization maintains conservation sites from Alaska to Hawaii, the sub-Arctic to the Gulf Coast. Apolitical and non-profit, Ducks Unlimited is, according to a national survey conducted in 1995 by the Angus Reid Group, "the nation's most trusted and respected conservation organization."

In 1938, Ed Russenholt defined conservation as "the use of all resources of land and water for the greatest good of the greatest number of people over the longest time." As Ducks Unlimited moves through its seventh decade, Russenholt's credo remains its mission.

BIRDS

B!RDS

FINE FEATHERED FRIENDS

"At sunset," said a Ducks Unlimited Greenwing leader, "you can stand outside Oak Hammock Marsh and watch geese fly overhead, covering the sky for 45 minutes."

In the autumn of 1997, Ducks Unlimited recorded the greatest migration in its history. More than one million ducks traveled through Canada to winter grounds in the southern United States and Mexico. Other air-borne travelers included geese, shorebirds, songbirds and raptors.

The great migration routes of North America are called flyways: the Pacific, from Alaska to Baja, California; the Central, from the Arctic to the Rio Grande; the Atlantic, from Labrador to Florida; and the most traveled, the Mississippi, from Hudson Bay to the Gulf of Mexico.

Some ancient people thought birds flew to the moon during migration. They don't fly that far or that high, but they do cover significant distances at impressive altitudes. The Arctic tern is circumpolar, traveling from the Arctic to the Antarctic. Barheaded geese cross the Himalayas at 29,500 feet (9,000 metres). Whooper swans en route from Iceland to western Europe have been tracked by airline pilots at 27,000 feet (8,230 metres). Mallard ducks have reached 21,000 feet (6,400 metres) and even the sparrow-size chaffinch is capable of soaring to 3,000 feet (1,000 metres).

Many birds make non-stop flights, adding body weight (up to 100 percent) and new feathers before setting off. The white-fronted goose migrates from Greenland to Scotland and Ireland (approximately 2,000 miles or 3,500 kilometres) in 48 hours.

There are also swimming and walking migrants. The ostrich, emu and Emperor penguin travel on foot; other penguins and auks travel by water. How do these birds find their way? By reading the stars, relying on the sun as a compass, tracking the earth's magnetism, and being guided by odours.

PROTECTING THE NESTING GROUNDS

Birds have continued to migrate between familial breeding and wintering grounds over the millennia, even as continents have drifted farther apart and ice ages have changed the topography. The great breeding ground for most North American waterfowl is the midwest prairie. Fifty percent of the continent's ducks are hatched on five percent of North America's nesting habitat – the Prairie pothole wetlands of Saskatchewan, Manitoba, Alberta and North and South Dakota.

Before 1960, birds had little trouble finding nesting cover, but, in recent times, conversion of wetlands and grasslands to croplands has reduced cover, allowing predators easy access to nests. Ducks Unlimited's Oak Hammock Marsh, more than 14 square miles (36 square kilometres) of marshes, meadows, tall grass prairie, lure crops and aspen-oak bluffs, encourages nesting. The Manitoba Wildlife Federation and DU volunteers build nesting structures from straw and wire, and mount them on metal poles, high above the water, safe from predators. The successful hatching rate for ducklings in these nests is 95 percent. Other ducks nest on the roof of the Oak Hammock Interpretive Centre, where native grasses have been planted.

WEBBED FEET, WONDROUS LEGENDS

Ducks are found worldwide, wherever they find water, from Tierra del Fuego, at the southern tip of South America, to the Arctic. Twenty-nine species breed in Canada, from Arctic sea-ducks to the clown-masked harlequin on the Atlantic and Pacific coasts. Ducks and geese have existed in virtually their present forms since at least the Cenozoic era, up to 100 million years ago. There are paintings of geese and ducks in Egyptian tombs. Donald Duck, however, did not arrive until 1934, and

Daffy didn't turn up until 1937 – same year as Ducks Unlimited.

All cultures have waterfowl myths and legends. In Russian fairy tales, swans and geese are often the rescuers of babies. Egyptian and Chinese legends saw geese as messengers between sky and earth. The duck was sacred to Aphrodite, Eros and Priapus, all gods of erotic love, and ancient Greeks believed ducks had aphrodisiac qualities. Greek women wore jewelry in the shape of ducks. In ancient China, a lover would send a duck or goose to his beloved, and a pair of geese was an appropriate gift for newlyweds, as geese tend to mate for life.

To Hindus, ducks, geese and swans were sacred water birds. Celts also believed geese to be sacred and took them to shrines. Ducks figure prominently in the myths of northwest Pacific coast indians, but not always favourably. In some legends, an incestuous brother is turned into a duck.

Swans have special – indeed, Royal – status in England. Since Tudor times, swans gliding along the Thames River have been deemed the property of the reigning monarch. The only exceptions are a number of swans allotted to the Worshipful Companies of Dyers and Vintners. Once a year, in July, Her Majesty's Swan Keeper leads a flotilla of skiffs upstream for a ceremony known as "swan-upping." Swan-upping is the marking of birds' beaks or webs to designate ownership. The Queen's scarlet-jerseyed swanherds no longer mark the birds, but the blue-topped Dyers and Vintners continue the ritual. If you are in London at 9:30 a.m. on Monday in the third week of July (any July – this has been going on since the 1500s) head for the Temple Steps at Blackfriars and observe. But don't get upped.

THE BIRTH OF BIRDS

The domestic ducks we know are all descendants of the wild mallard, familiar (in males) for its green head and white-ringed neck. The mallard, and all feathered creatures, are believed to be descended from a prehistoric creature known as *Archaeopteryx lithographica*, whose fossilized remains have been dated at 140 million years of age. This creature may have been the common ancestor of both birds and reptiles, or the link between them. The largest flying creature known to paleontologists is a winged reptile of the order *Quetzalcoatlus*, which glided over what is now Texas 70 million years ago on wings spanning more than 68 feet (20.7 metres) from tip to tip.

Ducks Unlimited and other conservationists are determined to keep today's species from becoming extinct. The worst example of species extinction in modern times is the elimination, in just thirty years, of the passenger pigeon. Species currently monitored with concern include the piping plover, peregrine falcon, bald eagle, least tern, pintail, harlequin duck and scaup. Results in some cases are encouraging. In 1941, there were only twenty whooping cranes in North America. By 1998, the number was estimated at 400.

We owe birds more than we can imagine, apart from their beauty and song. We owe them, among other things, the creation of the world's oldest art forms: architecture and dance. All architecture, from the teepee to the highrise loft, began with the nest. All dance, from aboriginal ceremonies to "Swan Lake" and "Firebird," began with the courting rituals of birds. Lord, luv a duck!

BIRD-WATCHING, BIRD NAMING

More than five centuries ago, Dame Juliana Berners published her "Book of St. Alban's." In it, she collected group names of animals—feathered, furred and human. Some of these collective names are well known—a pride of lions, a pack of wolves, a pod of whales. But others are arcane and fascinating and, often, extraordinarily apt. Some are surprising. For example, we have all heard of a gaggle of geese, but this term refers only to geese gathered on the ground. A group of geese in flight is called a skein.

Among the most felicitous terms:
- a charm of finches;
- a chattering of choughs;
- a kindle of kittens;
- a spring of teals;
- a bouquet of pheasants;
- a murmur of starlings;
- and, loveliest of all: an exaltation of larks.

A flock of ducks in flight is a team. A band of kangaroos is a troop. Leopards, not surprisingly, travel in leaps, but it seems odd to hear of a stud of mares.

Some others: a muster of peacocks, a bevy of quail, a fall of woodcock, a clamor of rooks, a covey of partridge, and a watch of nightingales. Moles are, apparently diligent; thus, a labor of moles. At the other extreme is a sloth of bears. And then there is a confusion of guinea fowl.

Some collective names are sinister. Besides the familiar pack of wolves, we have a gang of elks, a skulk of foxes, and, most menacing, a murder of crows. But others are the height of propriety and respectability. Among these: a bench of bishops, a congregation of plovers and a parliament of owls.

PHEASANT WITH NEWBURG SAUCE

Chicken or turkey breast can be substituted

4	boneless pheasant breast halves, skin on	4
	Salt and pepper	
2 Tbsp.	butter	30 mL
1 Tbsp.	olive oil	15 mL
2	garlic cloves, minced	2
1	leek, trimmed, thinly sliced	1
2 c.	sliced mixed mushrooms	500 mL
	(buttons, Shiitake, Portabellas, etc.)	
3 Tbsp.	flour	45 mL
1 c.	light cream	250 mL
1 1/2 c.	chicken broth	375 mL
1/4 tsp.	ground nutmeg	2 mL
1/4 c.	dry sherry	60 mL
	Salt and pepper, to taste	

Pat pheasant pieces dry; season well with salt and pepper. Heat butter and oil in large skillet over medium high until hot. Add breast pieces; brown on both sides for about 3-4 minutes per side. Remove and keep warm. Add garlic, leek and mushrooms to the remaining fat in the pan. Sauté, stirring occasionally, until mushrooms are slightly browned. Remove mushrooms and leeks from pan with a slotted spoon and reserve.

Add flour to liquid and fat remaining in the skillet; stir 1 minute to obtain a smooth roux. Gradually stir in cream and broth, stirring and cooking until sauce starts to thicken. Add nutmeg and sherry to pan. Return pheasant pieces, mushrooms and leeks to pan and mix well. Reduce heat to simmer and simmer 4-5 minutes or until heated through. Add a little more broth if you prefer the sauce to be thinner. Salt and pepper to taste before serving.

MAKES: 4 servings

Serving suggestion: Excellent with snow peas and whipped potatoes.

Wine suggestion: Buttery white: '96 Behringer Chardonnay, California $$$

QUAIL WITH SAGE, TOMATOES AND FRIED POLENTA

4 Cornish game hens or chicken pieces can be substituted

Quail

8	quail, washed, dried, trimmed of fat	8
1/4 c.	flour	60 mL
1/4 tsp.	*each* salt and pepper	2 mL
3 Tbsp.	olive oil	45 mL
1 1/2 c.	dry white wine	310 mL
3	shallots, finely chopped	3
2	garlic cloves, minced	2
2	large tomatoes, chopped	2
1 Tbsp.	chopped fresh sage (or 1 tsp./5 mL dried)	15 mL
	Salt and pepper, to taste	
	Fresh sage leaves	
1	recipe polenta (preferably made with Parmesan cheese)	

Pat birds dry with paper towel. Tie the legs together with wing tips underneath. Place flour, salt and pepper in a plastic bag. Shake birds or poultry pieces in bag until coated. In a large deep non-stick skillet over medium heat brown birds well on all sides, in batches, for 6-8 minutes. Transfer birds to a plate and keep warm. Pour off any drippings in the pan.

Stir wine, shallots, garlic, tomatoes and sage into skillet; boil 2 minutes. Add quail, reduce heat to medium low, cover and simmer, turning occasionally, for 20 minutes or until birds are tender. Remove birds to a platter to keep warm. Boil sauce over medium high, stirring occasionally for 8-10 minutes or until thickened slightly. Season to taste with salt and pepper.

While birds are cooking, cut polenta (homemade spread in a cookie sheet or purchased in a roll from a deli or supermarket) into triangles or other shapes. Heat a little oil in a large skillet and sauté the pieces, in batches, for 2-3 minutes or until nicely browned.

MAKES: 4 servings

Serving suggestion: Arrange birds, polenta pieces and sauce on a large platter; serve with a green vegetable such as broccoli.

Wine suggestion: Smooth earthy red: '95 Judot Bourgogne Pinot Noir, France $$

BIRDS

FIVE SPICE ROAST DUCK
WITH PLUM CHUTNEY

Plum Chutney

4 c.	halved, pitted plums (1 1/2 lb./750 g)	1 L
1	onion, chopped	1
1/2 c.	water	125 mL
1 tsp.	minced fresh ginger	5 mL
2	garlic cloves, minced	2
1/3 c.	sugar	75 mL
1/4 c.	cider vinegar	60 mL
1/2 tsp.	*each* ground cinnamon and coriander	3 mL
1/4 tsp.	salt	2 mL
1/8 tsp.	hot chili paste	0.5 mL

Roast Duck

4 1/2 lb.	duck	2 kg
1/8 tsp.	*each* salt and pepper	0.5 mL
1	orange, halved	1
2	green onions, cut-up	2
3	garlic cloves, halved	3
2 Tbsp.	Chinese five-spice powder	30 mL
1/2 c.	water	125 mL

Plum Chutney: in large, heavy saucepan, bring plums, onion, water, ginger and garlic to boil over medium heat; reduce heat to medium-low, cover and simmer, stirring occasionally for 30 minutes or until plums are tender.

Stir in sugar, vinegar, cinnamon, coriander, salt and hot chili paste. Bring to boil; reduce heat to low and simmer, stirring frequently, for 35 minutes or until mixture reaches consistency of thick sauce. (Cool, cover and refrigerate for up to 1 week or freeze for up to 2 months.) Makes about 2 1/2 c. (625 mL).

Roast Duck: Preheat oven to 450˚F. (230˚C). Rinse duck; wipe cavity and pat dry with paper towels. Sprinkle salt and pepper inside. Stuff orange halves, green onions and garlic into cavity. Skewer cavity closed. Using a sharp knife, prick duck all over, just through the skin. Rub duck all over with five-spice powder. Tie legs together. Fold wings behind to secure neck skin. Place duck, breast side up, on greased rack in roasting pan. Pour water into pan.

Place duck in oven; reduce heat to 350˚F. (180˚C) and roast for 20 minutes per pound (500 g) or until juices run clear when tested with knife, basting and repricking skin every 20 minutes. Remove duck from oven; tent with foil and let stand for 10 minutes before carving.

MAKES: 4 servings

Serving suggestion: Serve with plum chutney.

Wine suggestion: Round, spicy red: '96 Wynns Coonawarra Estate Shiraz, Australia $$

ROAST PHEASANT
WITH ORANGE ROSEMARY BUTTER

Chicken (whole or pieces) or Cornish game hens can be substituted for the pheasant. Whole roasted pheasant needs to be basted to keep the breast as moist as the rest of the bird.

1 Tbsp.	grainy Dijon mustard	15 mL
2 Tbsp.	orange juice	30 mL
2 tsp.	finely chopped orange peel	10 mL
3 Tbsp.	unsalted butter, softened	45 mL
4	garlic cloves, sliced	4
2 tsp.	finely chopped fresh rosemary Freshly ground black pepper	10 mL
1	(2 1/4 lb./1 kg) pheasant, cleaned, patted dry	1
3/4 c.	chicken broth	175 mL

For the baste: in a small bowl combine first 7 ingredients and blend well until the butter is incorporated.

Place bird in a large non-aluminum mixing bowl. Starting around the main body cavity, carefully slip your hand under the skin, making sure not to break it. (You may need to use gloves if you have long fingernails.) Smooth the butter mixture all over the bird both under the skin and on top of the skin. Cover bird and let stand for up to 8 hours in the refrigerator.

Preheat oven to 425ºF. (220ºC). Place bird, breast side up, in a roasting pan on a rack or on a vertical roaster. Add chicken broth to bottom of pan. Roast bird for 45 minutes to 1 hour, or until juices run clear when thigh is pierced with a knife. Halfway through cooking, baste bird. Cover bird; let rest for 10 minutes before carving.

Cut bird in half; arrange on a serving platter; pour some of the juices over and serve immediately.

MAKES: 2 servings

Serving suggestion: Serve on buttered noodles with an orange spinach salad.

Wine suggestion: Complex white:
'95 Hardy "Eileen Hardy"
Chardonnay,
Australia $$$

CURRIED PARTRIDGES

Quail, small Cornish game hens, chicken or turkey pieces can be substituted.

4	partridges, cleaned, dried, halved	4
1 1/2 c.	plain yogurt	375 mL
1 Tbsp.	grated fresh ginger	15 mL
5	garlic cloves, minced	5
1 1/2 tsp.	salt	8 mL
1 1/2 tsp.	garum masala*	8 mL
1 1/2 tsp.	turmeric	8 mL
1 1/2 tsp.	ground coriander	8 mL
1 1/2 tsp.	ground cumin	8 mL
3/4 tsp.	cayenne	4 mL
3 Tbsp.	unsalted butter	45 mL
3	large onions, very thinly sliced	3
1 Tbsp.	packed brown sugar	15 mL
2 c.	dried apricot halves	500 mL
3	large ripe tomatoes, seeded, chopped	3
1 c.	chicken broth	250 mL

** A spice blend found in ethnic sections of most supermarkets*

Halve small birds (or use chicken pieces); place in large bowl. Combine following 9 ingredients, mixing well. Add to birds; turn several times to fully coat all pieces. Set aside 3/4 hour. Heat butter in large skillet until hot. Add partridge halves, draining off marinade. Sear on both sides until nicely browned. Place in bottom of a large casserole with a lid. Preheat oven to 350ºF. (180ºC). Add onions and sugar to the hot skillet; cook over medium-high heat, stirring occasionally until onions have caramelized and are very soft. Add apricot halves, tomatoes and the broth mixed with the marinade. Heat 1 minute before pouring over birds in casserole. Mix gently. Cover and bake 1 hour.

MAKES: 4 servings

Serving suggestion: Serve with hot Basmati rice and a steamed green vegetable such as broccoli.

Wine suggestion: Smooth, rich red: '94 Regaleali Conte Tasca D'Almerita, Italy $$

SAUTÉED DUCK BREASTS WITH RASPBERRY VINEGAR SAUCE

Chicken or turkey pieces or pheasant breasts can be substituted for the duck breasts.

4	boneless duck breast halves with skin on	4
Marinade		
3	garlic cloves, minced	3
1 Tbsp.	olive oil	15 mL
2 Tbsp.	raspberry or Balsamic vinegar	30 mL
Sauce		
2 Tbsp.	unsalted butter, softened, divided	30 mL
2	medium shallots, minced	2
1/2 c.	*each* beef or duck broth *and* red wine	125 mL
2 Tbsp.	raspberry or Balsamic vinegar	30 mL
1 tsp.	tomato paste	5 mL
	Salt and freshly ground black pepper	

In a small bowl, combine marinade ingredients. Pound breast halves between two pieces of wax paper to evenly flatten. Score flattened duck breasts with a very sharp knife by cutting crisscross lines on the skin, making sure not to cut into the duck meat. (Chicken, turkey or pheasant will not need scoring.) Place breasts in a large plastic sealable bag; pour in marinade. Marinate 1-4 hours, refrigerated, turning occasionally.

Remove breasts from marinade. Heat 1 Tbsp. (15 mL) butter in a large skillet on medium-high; sauté breasts, skin side down for about 5-7 minutes. Turn over and sauté for another 4-6 minutes or until duck breasts are medium rare and chicken, turkey or pheasant breasts are fully cooked. Remove to a side plate; cover.

Discard all but 2 Tbsp. (30 mL) of drippings; sauté shallots for a minute or until softened. Add broth, red wine, vinegar and tomato paste on medium-high heat. Reduce mixture to a light glaze, approximately 5 minutes. Whisk in remaining butter to thicken and add a sheen. Season to taste.

MAKES: 4 servings

Serving suggestion: Slice breasts on the diagonal and arrange on serving plates. Drizzle with sauce and serve immediately with wild rice and sautéed Savoy cabbage.

Wine suggestion: Rich, minty red: '96 Cape Mentelle Shiraz, Australia $$

ROAST GOOSE WITH CORNBREAD, FRUIT AND CHESTNUT STUFFING

1 turkey or 2 (4-5 lb./2-2.5 kg) ducks can be substituted

2 Tbsp.	*each* olive oil and unsalted butter	30 mL
1	medium onion, chopped	1
1/2 lb.	mushrooms, sliced	250 g
2	celery stalks, chopped	2
1 c.	coarsely chopped cooked (or canned) chestnuts	250 mL
1/2 c.	*each* coarsely chopped, dried apricots and dried prunes	125 mL
2 tsp.	finely chopped fresh thyme	10 mL
4 c.	cubed dried-out cornbread	1 L
1/2 c.	chopped fresh parsley	125 mL
	Salt and coarse black pepper	
1	(8-10 lb./4-5 kg) goose	1
	Salt and coarse black pepper	

In a large skillet, heat oil and butter on medium heat; sauté onion for 5 minutes or until softened. Add mushrooms and celery; sauté until mushrooms are softened, about 4 minutes. Transfer to a large bowl. Add chestnuts, apricots, prunes, thyme, cornbread and parsley; mix well. Season to taste with salt and pepper. Cool.

Preheat oven to 450°F. (180°C). Clean and season the goose generously with salt and pepper inside and out. Prick skin with a metal skewer (not piercing the meat). Loosely pack stuffing into both cavities; secure by trussing with skewers or string. Place, breast side up, on a rack in a large roasting pan. Pour 2 c. (500 mL) water into pan. Steam, covered, for 1 hour. After 1/2 hour, check to make sure there is enough water, adding more if necessary. After the hour, remove most of the fat from the pan with a baster.

Add another 1 c. (250 mL) water to pan and discard cover. Lower oven to 375° F. (190°C). Continue roasting for about 1 1/2 hours more, basting with some red currant jelly mixed with a little water, if desired during the final hour (about 3 times). (If you are cooking 2 ducks, follow the same directions but reduce steaming to 1/2 hour and roasting to about 1 hour. Turkey should not be pricked and should be cooked slightly less than the goose.) Internal temperature for any of the birds should be 170° F. (80°C).

MAKES: 6 servings

Serving suggestion: Slice goose; serve with stuffing and Cumberland Sauce if desired.

Wine suggestion: Broad aromatic white: '95 Pierre Sparr Reserve Gewurztraminer, Alsace, France $$

Duck Salad with Wild Rice and Oranges

Chicken or turkey meat can be substituted.

Vinaigrette

3 Tbsp.	red wine vinegar	45 mL
1 Tbsp.	Dijon mustard	15 mL
1/3 c.	olive oil	75 mL
2	green onions, thinly sliced	2
	Salt and pepper, to taste	

Salad

1	4 1/2 lb. (2 kg) duck, quartered	1
3	garlic cloves, peeled, halved	3
	Salt and pepper	
1/3 c.	coarsely chopped toasted walnuts	75 mL
1/3 c.	finely diced celery	75 mL
1 Tbsp.	butter or margarine	15 mL
2	medium shallots, finely chopped	2
1/2 c.	wild rice, washed, drained	125 mL
2 c.	chicken broth	500 mL
1/2 lb.	mushrooms, thinly sliced	250 g
2 1/2	medium oranges, peeled, sectioned, roughly chopped	2 1/2

To make the vinaigrette, combine vinegar and mustard; whisk in oil; add green onions. Season to taste with salt and pepper. Reserve.

Preheat oven to 425ºF. (220ºC). Prick skin of duck all over. (Do not pierce meat.) Push halved garlic cloves and salt and pepper under skin. Put quarters on a rack in a roasting pan. Pour 1 c. (250 mL) water into pan; roast 30 minutes. Turn duck; roast 30-45 minutes longer or until the juices run clear when thigh is pierced with a knife. Allow to cool. Remove skin and garlic pieces. Cut meat into 1/2 " (1.25 cm) pieces. Combine in a medium bowl with walnuts, celery and 1/4 c. (60 mL) vinaigrette, tossing to coat all ingredients. Refrigerate for 2-4 hours or until ready to serve.

Meanwhile, melt butter in a medium saucepan until hot; add shallots; sauté over low heat until soft and transparent. Add rinsed and drained rice to pan; mix. Stir in broth; cover; simmer about 30-35 minutes, or until liquid is absorbed and rice is tender but still a bit crunchy. Cool. Add rice, mushrooms, oranges and remaining vinaigrette to duck salad in bowl. Mix well. Season with salt and pepper to taste.

MAKES: 4 to 6 servings

Serving suggestion: Just before serving, line plates with red lettuce. Mound duck salad on top; garnish with extra orange segments and parsley.

Wine suggestion: Complex champagne: '90 Veuve Clicquot Ponsardin Vintage Brut, France $$$

PHEASANT/DUCK BREASTS IN BLACK BEAN COMPOTE

Duck, pheasant, chicken, Cornish game hen and turkey breasts all work well.

1¹/2 lb.	breast meat pieces (duck, pheasant, etc.)	750 g
2 tsp.	cumin seeds	10 mL
4	slices lean bacon, diced	4
1	red onion, diced	1
4	garlic cloves, minced	4
1	small green bell pepper, seeded, diced	1
1	large carrot, peeled, diced	1
1	(19 fl. oz./540 mL) tin black beans, rinsed, drained	1
2 Tbsp.	chopped cilantro	30 mL
1 tsp.	Tabasco	5 mL
	Grated peel of 1 lime	
	Juice of 1/2 lime	
1	(10 fl. oz./284 mL) tin chicken broth	1

Half-cook the breast pieces by barbecuing, baking, microwaving (chicken and turkey only) or broiling.

Place a heavy skillet over medium heat until hot. Add cumin seeds; toss about 1 minute or until fragrant and starting to colour.

Remove. Add diced bacon to skillet; cook until crisp; remove.

Add diced onion, garlic, green pepper and carrot to fat in pan. Cook, stirring occasionally, until vegetables are softening. Add drained beans, bacon, cumin seed, cilantro, Tabasco, peel, juice and broth. Mix well. Cook another 1-2 minutes, mashing slightly with a potato masher as you cook. (The sauce should be slightly mashed but not puréed.) Add meat pieces; stir to cover meat with compote. Reduce heat to medium; cook 20-30 minutes.

MAKES: 4 servings

Serving suggestion: Serve with noodles or garlic mashed potatoes and a green vegetable. Another option: use the black bean compote without meat as a vegetarian dish over rice.

Wine suggestion: Earthy, complex red: '95 Robert Mondavi Napa Reserve Pinot Noir, California $$$

NOTE: If you would like to reduce the fat, remove the skin from the meat pieces before adding to the compote.

BRAISED GROUSE WITH CHORIZO, RAISINS AND ALMONDS

Cornish game hens, chicken pieces, rabbit, or partridge can be substituted. Grouse is a very strong earthy-flavoured game bird. This spicy Mexican style preparation helps balance the gaminess.

1/3 c.	dry sherry	75 mL
3 Tbsp.	golden raisins	45 mL
1/2 lb.	Chorizo sausage, casings removed	250 g
2 Tbsp.	vegetable oil	30 mL
4	grouse (3/4 lb./375 g each), well cleaned	4
1	medium onion, thinly sliced	1
2	Serraño chiles, seeded, finely chopped	2
1¹/4 c.	chicken broth	310 mL
1 lb.	tomatoes, peeled, seeded, puréed*	500 g
2	medium garlic cloves, minced	2
	Salt, to taste	
1/4 c.	lime juice	60 mL
1/2 lb.	carrots, peeled, julienned	250 g
1/2 lb.	zucchini, julienned into 2" (5 cm) lengths	250 g
2 Tbsp.	slivered almonds, toasted	30 mL

**Tins of puréed tomatoes can be substituted.*

In a small saucepan, heat sherry. Pour sherry over the raisins in a small bowl; cover; leave 2 - 4 hours.

In a large Dutch oven over medium-high heat, sauté chorizo until brown, about 5 minutes, breaking up pieces with a fork. Remove; drain on paper towels; reserve. Discard drippings from pan. In same pan, heat oil over medium-high. Add grouse; brown well on all sides, about 5-7 minutes. Remove from pan and reserve.

Add onion and chiles to pan; cook about 5 minutes or until soft. Add broth, stirring and scraping bits from the bottom of pan; bring to the boil; boil for 1 minute. Add tomatoes, garlic and salt; cook 2 more minutes over medium-high. Add chorizo, lime juice, and grouse. Cover and simmer 1 hour, on medium-low, basting birds every 15 minutes with sauce and vegetables. Add sherry that the raisins soaked in, carrots, and zucchini; mix to combine; simmer , uncovered, another 15 minutes or until grouse and vegetables are tender. Add almonds and raisins. Season to taste.

MAKES: 4 servings

Serving suggestion: Serve with an avocado and Romaine salad.

Wine suggestion: Big, peppery red: '95 Dry Creek Old Vines Reserve Zinfandel, California $$$

GRILLED MARINATED QUAIL

Any whole or cut-up poultry can be substituted. Quail are very delicate in flavour. Marinating them in a simple oil and vinegar preparation brings out their unique flavour. Plan on 4 per person for a main course or 2 per person for a first course. This recipe doubles or triples well. Other herbs that work nicely include basil, sage and rosemary.

Marinade

1	garlic clove, minced	1
1	shallot, finely chopped	1
1 Tbsp.	red wine vinegar	15 mL
2 Tbsp.	olive oil	30 mL
	Salt	
	Freshly ground black pepper	
1/4 tsp.	dried oregano	2 mL
1/4 tsp.	dried thyme	2 mL
4	(4 oz./125 g) quail	4

Combine all marinade ingredients in a bowl large enough to fit the quail. Marinate quail for 2-4 hours, covered, in the refrigerator. Turn several times.

Prepare barbecue, broiler or grill for medium-high cooking. Cook quail about 10 minutes, turning to evenly brown. Check breast meat to make sure it is just cooked through and not pink; and juices should run clear when thigh is pricked with a knife. Serve immediately.

MAKES: 1 serving as a main course or 2 servings as a first course

Serving suggestion: Serve with braised spinach and baby roasted potatoes for a main course.

Wine suggestion: Crisp, nervy white: '95 Chateâu de Cruzeau Graves, Bordeaux, France $$

Ducks Unlimited Canada's habitat programs are guided by a Continental Conservation Plan, which was developed in 1994 by senior biologists with DU Canada, DU Inc. (U.S.) and DUMAC (Mexico). The Plan contains a detailed analysis of the status of North American waterfowl species and their habitats, and provides recommendations regarding where and on what DU should focus its limited resources to provide maximum benefits for North American waterfowl populations.

ALMOND COATED LIVER
WITH TOMATO AND BASIL SAUCE

This recipe works well with duck, chicken, turkey or calves' liver.

1/3 c.	dried fine bread crumbs	75mL
1/3 c.	finely chopped toasted almonds	75mL
1 Tbsp.	dried basil	15mL
1/2 tsp.	*each* salt and coarse black pepper	3mL
1	egg, beaten with a little water	1
1¹/₂ lbs.	liver(s)	750g
8	slices lean maple or apple smoked bacon	8
2 Tbsp.	olive oil	30mL
1	medium onion, chopped	1
6	large garlic cloves, minced	6
1	(28 fl.oz./796 mL) tin diced plum tomatoes	1
3 Tbsp.	bottled chili sauce	45mL
	Salt and pepper, to taste	
2/3 c.	packed roughly chopped fresh basil leaves	150 mL

Combine the first 5 ingredients in a plastic bag, mixing well. Beat egg with water and place in a shallow bowl. Trim all fat and sinews from the chosen liver(s). Cook bacon in a hot skillet until nicely browned; remove and keep warm. Keep bacon fat remaining in the pan at a medium-high heat. Dip the liver slices or pieces in the beaten egg and then shake in the crumb mixture in the bag. When totally coated, drop into the hot fat. Cook on both sides for only a minute or two each side; so that the liver stays medium-rare in the centre. Remove liver(s) to keep warm with the bacon. Add the oil to the hot skillet. When hot, add onion and garlic, stirring and browning for 1-2 minutes. Add tomatoes, chili sauce, salt and pepper. Keep over medium-high heat for 3-5 minutes or until moisture is reduced and tomatoes start to thicken. Stir in basil. Remove from heat.

MAKES: 4 servings

Serving suggestion: Place a dollop of the tomato sauce on each hot dinner plate, top with the livers and two slices of bacon. Excellent with a sweet potato croquette or polenta and a green vegetable.

Wine suggestion: Spicy, ripe red: '92 Julian Chivite 125 Collection Red Reserva, Spain $$

PHEASANT CASSEROLE WITH MASCARPONE AND MUSHROOMS

Quail, partridge halves, Cornish game hens halves, chicken or turkey pieces can be substituted.

2	pheasants, cleaned, dried, cut in pieces	2
1	(10 fl. oz./284 mL) tin chicken broth	1
2 Tbsp.	olive oil	30 mL
1	large onion, thinly sliced	1
1	large leek, well-cleaned, thinly sliced	1
2 tsp	minced garlic	10 mL
3	Portabella mushrooms, coarsely chopped	3
1	(10 fl. oz./284 mL) tin Cream of Wild Mushroom soup	1
1/2 lb.	Mascarpone cheese	250 g
1/4 c.	dry sherry	60 mL
1½ Tbsp.	minced fresh rosemary	25 mL
	Salt and pepper, to taste	
1 c.	fresh whole wheat bread crumbs	250 mL
3 Tbsp.	minced fresh parsley	45 mL
2 tsp.	minced fresh garlic	10 mL
	Grated peel of 1 large lemon	

Preheat oven to 350ºF. (180ºC). Place meat pieces in a large casserole; cover with broth. Cover; bake 30 minutes. Remove; drain and reserve broth.

Meanwhile, heat oil in large skillet. Add onion, leek, garlic and Portabellas; cook until vegetables start to soften. Add to meat in casserole. In a medium bowl mix together the soup, Mascarpone, reserved cooking broth, sherry and rosemary. Sprinkle with salt and pepper. Pour mixture over ingredients in casserole. Mix gently to combine. Place in oven, uncovered, for 30 minutes. Mix together crumbs, parsley, garlic and lemon peel. Spread over top of casserole. Return to oven for another 15 minutes. Broil briefly if you prefer the topping to be more crisp.

MAKES: 4 servings

Serving suggestion: Serve over noodles or rice so the ample amount of sauce can coat.

Wine suggestion: Toasty white: '96 Loius Latour Chardonnay Grande Ardèche, France $$

NOTE: Mascarpone is a mild cream cheese usually available in tubs. Any good quality cream cheese (not "light") can be substituted.

BRAISED GOOSE WITH ROOT VEGETABLES AND OLIVES

2 small ducks or Cornish game hens can be substituted.

1	goose, (about 8-11 lb./4-5 kg), cut into 10-12 pieces *(wing tips, bones, fat and skin removed)*	1
	Salt and freshly ground black pepper	
2 Tbsp.	olive oil	30 mL
2	onions, thinly sliced	2
1½ lb.	turnips or rutabaga, peeled, cut into 3/4" (1.85 cm) dice	750 g
2	carrots, peeled, sliced	2
1 lb.	parsnips, peeled, cut into 3/4" (1.85 cm) dice	500 g
8	garlic cloves, minced	8
4 c.	tinned, diced plum tomatoes with juice	1 L
2 c.	white wine	500 mL
1 c.	pitted green Sicilian olives, drained	250 mL
1 Tbsp.	finely chopped fresh thyme or 1½ tsp. (8 mL) dried	15 mL
1	(28 fl. oz./796 mL) tin chicken broth	1
1/4 c.	chopped fresh parsley (optional)	60 mL

Season goose pieces with salt and pepper in a bowl. In a very large heavy casserole, heat oil on medium-high; brown goose on all sides, in batches, about 5-7 minutes. Remove; reserve.

Discard all but 1/4 c. (60 mL) fat. Add onion; cook 5-7 minutes or until lightly browned. Add turnips, carrots, parsnips; cook another 2 minutes, stirring to coat vegetables. Add garlic; cook 1 minute. Add tomatoes, wine, olives, thyme and broth; bring to a boil. Add goose pieces to casserole, arranging around vegetables. Reduce heat; cover; simmer until goose pieces are tender, about 1 1/2 hours. After 45 minutes, stir well.

Using a slotted spoon, transfer goose pieces and vegetables to a large platter; cover. Remove fat from pan juices with a "wand" or divided cup specially made for the purpose; pour juices into a medium saucepan. Reduce over high heat, about 7 minutes. Season to taste. Spoon sauce over goose and vegetables. Garnish with fresh thyme branches and parsley if desired.

MAKES: 6-8 servings

Serving suggestion: Serve with hot French bread.

Wine suggestion: Smooth, dense red: '94 Miguel Torres "Don Miguel Reserva Especial" Spain, $$

DUCK SAUSAGE PATTIES WITH APPLE CRANBERRY GINGER RELISH

Ground pork, chicken, turkey, venison, buffalo or a combination of meats can be substituted.

Relish

3	large tart apples, peeled, cored, diced	3
3/4 c.	dried cranberries	175 mL
1 Tbsp.	minced fresh ginger	15 mL
1/4 c.	packed brown sugar	60 mL
2 Tbsp.	cider vinegar	30 mL
1/4 tsp.	ground cinnamon	1 mL
1/8 tsp.	*each* ground cloves and mace	0.5 mL
1¹/₂ c.	water	375 mL

Sausage

1 lb.	*each* boneless duck breast and pork sausage	500g
2 Tbsp.	oil	30 mL
1	large onion, finely chopped	1
3	garlic cloves, minced	3
1/2 c.	*each* tawny port and chopped pistachio nuts	125 mL
1¹/₂ tsp.	salt	8 mL
1/2 tsp.	black pepper	3 mL
1/4 tsp.	dried thyme	1 mL
1/2 c.	finely chopped parsley	125 mL

Relish: in a large saucepan, combine all relish ingredients on medium. Stir; cook, uncovered, 20-25 minutes or until apples begin to break down but still have some shape. Taste for seasoning; cool.

The sausage: remove skin from the duck breast; cut skin into 2" (5 cm) pieces. Cut duck meat into 2" (5 cm) pieces. In a food processor fitted with a metal blade, process duck skin. Add meat and process until ground. In a large bowl, combine ground duck and sausage. Set aside. (Using the skin is optional.)

In a medium skillet, heat oil on medium; cook onion until softened and lightly browned, about 5-7 minutes. Add garlic; cook 1 minute. Add port and nuts; bring to a boil; cook 1-2 minutes. Cool. Add cooled onion mixture and remaining ingredients to meat mixture; mix well. Make into patties; cover; refrigerate overnight.

To cook, heat a large nonstick skillet on medium-high and cook sausage patties about 2-4 minutes each side. Serve with the relish.

MAKES: 6-8 servings

Serving suggestion: A spectacular brunch with scrambled eggs and home-fried potatoes.

Wine suggestion: Robust rosé: '96 Joseph Phelps Grenache Rosé, California $$

MARINATED PARTRIDGE
WITH APPLE-PEAR-
DRIED CHERRY COMPOTE

Grouse, chicken, or Cornish game hens can be substituted.

Marinade

1	shallot, finely chopped	1
1	garlic clove, minced	1
1 Tbsp.	*each* Balsamic vinegar and soy sauce	15 mL
1 Tbsp.	molasses	15 mL
	Freshly ground black pepper	
2 Tbsp.	olive oil	30 mL
4	(3/4 lb./375 g each) partridge, well cleaned, rinsed, dried	4
1/2 c.	water	125 mL

Compote

1	tart apple, peeled, cored, finely diced	1
1	Anjou or Bosc pear, peeled, cored, finely diced	1
1/2 c.	dried cherries	125 mL
2 Tbsp.	packed brown sugar	30 mL
1 Tbsp.	cider vinegar	15 mL
1/8 tsp.	cinnamon	1 mL
1 c.	water	250 mL

In a large bowl, whisk together shallot, garlic, Balsamic vinegar, soy sauce, molasses, and pepper. Pour in olive oil in a steady stream while whisking until completely blended. Taste for seasoning. (A food processor can also be used.)

Place partridges in marinade; turn birds over to evenly coat. Cover, refrigerate and marinate for 2-4 hours.

Preheat oven to 350ºF. (180ºC). Place partridges in a roasting pan and pour excess marinade over them. Add the 1/2 c. (125 mL) water; cover pan with foil; roast for about 1 hour or until the birds are tender and juices run clear when pierced with a knife.

Compote: in a small saucepan over medium heat, combine all ingredients. Stir to mix well. Cook until fruit begins to break down, about 20-25 minutes, stirring occasionally. (Adjust the sweetness by adding more brown sugar, if desired.) Remove from heat and keep covered.

Place birds on a platter. Pour over pan drippings and serve with lukewarm compote.

MAKES: 4 servings

Serving suggestion: Delicious with garlic mashed sweet potatoes and broccoli.

Wine suggestion: Smoky ripe red: '96 Chapoutier Le Bernardine Chateâuneuf du Pape, France $$$

GAME

GAME

WHO'S WHO IN THE MARSH

If Ducks Unlimited had a guest list for wetlands visitors, it would include far more than ducks. Among the creatures sharing the food, water and shelter of Ducks Unlimited habitats are moose, muskrats, beavers, foxes, coyotes, and white-tailed deer. Elk, caribou, rabbits, squirrels, antelope – all manner of mammals are protected by Ducks Unlimited programs.

When Ducks Unlimited began its work in Canada, at the end of the 1930s, there were still great herds of buffalo roaming the plains. Their descendants are now in Elk Island National Park, east of Edmonton; Wood Buffalo National Park, straddling the border of Alberta and the Northwest Territories; Winnipeg Zoo, and parts of the United States. At Oak Hammock Marsh, buffalo skulls are still found, along with various fossils.

Of all North America's large animals, the most numerous is the white-tailed deer, which – unless depleted by severe winters – can double its population in a single year. Whitetail fawns are born usually as twins, weighing as little as 4.4 pounds (two kilograms), but growing to 242 pounds (110 kilograms) in a year. Two hundred years ago, there were few whitetails in Canada, but forest cutting, the reduction of predator activity, and prairie fire control have expanded their territory. Now they roam through forest and brush areas from Canada's Maritime provinces to British Columbia and from Central America to the far north.

Bears of all kinds – brown, grizzly, even polar – are beneficiaries of Ducks Unlimited habitat programs. Bears particularly like bogs, because that's where blueberries and cranberries grow. Bears are great berry fanciers. The bear is notorious for his sweet tooth, and has the cavities to prove it.

The massive bull moose – taller than a horse, weighing up to 1,800 pounds (810 kilograms) and crowned by antlers that can spread six feet (1.8 metres) is a herbivore. The moose consumes vast quantities of upland and wetland vegetation – up to 60 pounds (27 kilograms) a day in summer – often diving deep under water to reach particularly succulent plants. Despite its delicate diet, the moose is a tough customer. A single moose, wielding lethal hooves and antlers, can protect itself from a pack of wolves.

Wolves travel in packs of as many as 20 animals, led by the alpha male and alpha female, strongest and wisest of the pack. They hunt together, chasing and circling their prey – moose, deer, elk, caribou. An adult wolf is about the size of a German shepherd – up to 130 pounds (59 kilograms) – and extraordinarily powerful. It can run for hours and can leap 15 feet (4.5 metres). Coyotes, part of the same canine family, can reach a speed of 40 miles (60 kilometres) an hour. All wild dogs – wolves, coyotes, foxes – are superb swimmers.

And then there are North America's wild cats – the cougar, bobcat and lynx. Cougars, also known as mountain lions, pumas and panthers, are the biggest, fastest cats on the continent. Males weigh up to 160 pounds (73 kilograms). They hunt deer in mountains and forests along the Pacific coast from Canada to Mexico. The lynx – sometimes called the ghost of the forest – lives in cold northern areas of Canada and the United States. Smaller than the cougar, weighing not more than 25 pounds (11 kilograms), the lynx hunts snowshoe hares, and may feast on as many as 200 a year. Smallest of the wildcats is the bobcat, 22 pounds (10 kilograms) at its largest. Mainly a prowler of the eastern and central United States, the bobcat hunts rabbits, other small animals, and birds.

CARIBOU ENCOUNTER

In the summer of 1997, a Winnipeg decorative painter named Sandra Bacon, bored with the urban scene, called on her mother for a crash course in bread-baking and then traveled to the Northwest Territories to cook at an outcamp named Windy

River, most northerly of the Neultin Lake fly-in fishing lodges.

Accompanied by the black Labrador she had bought at a Ducks Unlimited auction (and named Micaela Cameron, after her maternal grandmother) she flew into the wild, remote country where the legendary trapper Ragnar Jonsson lived alone with his husky dogs for 43 years.

"It was," she said, "the most fascinating adventure. Bald eagles overhead. Tiny, beautiful tundra birds. Grizzly bears. This was their turf, they had owned it for thousands of years. And I was on it."

And then came the caribou. "I was up at 5:45 am, starting the generator for breakfast, when I saw this huge shape in the water." The huge shape was a caribou, a strong swimmer using its hooves as paddles. Only one was visible, but later, a long line of caribou could be seen moving single file along the horizon across the bay. Setting out in boats, fishing lodge guests saw thousands of caribou – an endless line – on their southward journey.

"They came through in herds, dawn 'til dusk," said Ms. Bacon. "It was the most elegant animal I've ever seen, with huge racks, and smooth, silent movements. And they were curious about us, too, circling and watching."

At night, the howls of the wolf pack trailing the caribou were heard across the bay. A wolf needs 11 to 14 caribou a year for its food supply, but caribou are faster than wolves, and hard to catch, unless chased in relays, ambushed, or caught at vulnerable times.

After 10 days, the migrating herd had passed through the Windy River camp. "They just vanished," said Ms. Bacon. "Our pilots looked for them from the air, but there was no sight of them. That August coming of the caribou was magical...mystical."

FOILING THE FOX

Animals whose numbers have increased substantially in recent years are small predators. There are probably more foxes skulking through North America than ever before, preying on nesting birds and other small ground-dwellers. The cat-like red fox (which can also be cross-coloured, black and silver) thrives in clearcuts, farmlands, orchards and golf courses. You may even see one prowling through your suburban backyard. By restoring large blocks of grassland around wetlands, Ducks Unlimited provides protection for ground-nesting birds. Predator-proof innovations like brooding islands and elevated nests also foil foxes and their feral friends.

ANIMALS ON FOUR LEGS AND TWO

The bond between humans and other animals is historic and intense, ranging from cooperative work to recreation, affection to worship. An oblique suggestion of the value of finned, feathered and furry friends is their appearance on currency, from the US buffalo nickel to the bear, bobcat, mackerel, dove and other creatures on Canadian coins and bills.

The tree of life is thought to have begun with a universal ancestor, a single-cell microbe, more than 3.5 billion years ago. Earth itself, host for evolving life, is believed to have been formed from the dust of a star – all of which recent scientific theory gives new resonance to the story of the creation of the first human – Adam – from dust.

In "The Phenomenon of Man," first published in Paris in 1955, Teilhard de Chardin wrote "All living creatures, from the humblest bacteria to man, contain exactly the same complicated types of vitamins and enzymes...Life was born and propogates itself on the earth as a solitary pulsation."

This is a remarkable concept. Most of us probably don't object to being six degrees of separation from royalty, but six degrees from a salamander?

Well, perhaps more than six. But in Père Teilhard's compound of science and philosophy, there is the healthy notion that all of us – animals, plants, human beings – are parts of the same ecosystem, dependent on one another for survival.

GRILLED BUFFALO STEAKS WITH JALAPENO BUTTER

Beef steaks can be substituted

Fire Herb Butter

1/3 c.	butter, softened	75 mL
1	garlic clove, minced	1
1	Jalapeño chile, seeded and minced	1
2 Tbsp.	chopped fresh coriander	30 mL
2 Tbsp.	chopped fresh mint	30 mL
1/4 tsp.	*each* salt and pepper	1 mL

Red Wine Marinade

1/3 c.	dry red wine	75 mL
3 Tbsp.	Balsamic vinegar	45 mL
2	garlic cloves, minced	2
2	shallots, minced	2
1 Tbsp.	chopped fresh rosemary (or 1 tsp./5 mL dried)	15 mL
1 Tbsp.	Dijon mustard	15 mL
1/2 tsp.	pepper	3 mL
1/2 c.	olive oil	125 mL
4	New York strip buffalo steaks, 3/4" (1.85 cm) thick	4

Fire Herb Butter: in small bowl, combine all ingredients. (Butter can be covered and refrigerated up to 5 days.)

Red Wine Marinade: in a small bowl, whisk together wine, vinegar, garlic, shallots, rosemary, mustard and pepper. Gradually whisk in oil. Place steaks in a sealable plastic bag, pour in marinade, turn steaks to coat completely. Cover and refrigerate for at least 6 hours or up to 24 hours, turning steaks occasionally. Let stand at room temperature 30 minutes before grilling.

Prepare barbecue, broiler or grill to medium-high heat. Reserving marinade, place steaks on greased grill or broiler pan; cook, brushing with marinade, for 2-3 minutes per side for medium rare. Transfer to plate; cover with foil and let stand 5 minutes before serving. Discard any unused marinade.

MAKES: 4 servings

Serving suggestion: Serve each steak with a dollop of room temperature Fire Herb Butter along with baked potatoes and grilled vegetables.

Wine suggestion: Meaty red: '95 Antinori Peppoli Chianti Classico, Italy $$

MEDITERRANEAN BRAISED RABBIT WITH FENNEL AND OLIVES

Chicken pieces (same weight) can be substituted. Remove skin before starting recipe.

4 3/4 lb.	rabbit pieces	2.4 kg
1/4 c.	flour	60 mL
4 sl.	bacon, cut into 1/2" (1.25 cm) pieces	4 sl.
2 Tbsp.	olive oil	30 mL
1	onion, chopped	1
8	garlic cloves, quartered	8
1	large fennel bulb, halved and thickly sliced	1
1	bay leaf	1
1 Tbsp.	*each* fresh chopped oregano, rosemary and thyme	15 mL
1/4 tsp.	pepper	1 mL
4 c.	chicken broth	4 L
2/3 c.	orange juice	150 mL
1 Tbsp.	grated orange peel	15 mL
1 c.	marinated green or black olives	250 mL
1/4 c.	chopped fresh parsley	60 mL

Dredge rabbit pieces in flour, shaking off excess flour, set aside.

In large, heavy Dutch oven, cook bacon over medium-high for 7 minutes or until browned and crisp. Using slotted spoon, transfer bacon to bowl.

Add oil to Dutch oven; cook rabbit, in batches, for 2 minutes per side or until browned. Transfer to plate. Drain off all but 1 Tbsp. (15 mL) of the drippings. Add onion and garlic; cook 5 minutes or until softened. Stir in fennel, bay leaf, oregano, rosemary, thyme, pepper, broth, orange juice and peel. Bring to a boil; reduce heat to medium-low and simmer, covered, for 45 minutes. Uncover and simmer 30 minutes longer or until meat is tender and nearly falling off the bones. Transfer rabbit to bowl; cover to keep warm.

Increase heat to high and boil broth, stirring occasionally, for 15 minutes or until reduced and slightly thickened; remove bay leaf. Add rabbit along with olives to broth; reduce heat to medium and simmer for 3-5 minutes or until heated through.

MAKES: 8 servings

Serving suggestion: Serve topped with the chopped bacon and parsley along with buttered egg noodles.

Wine suggestion: Grassy big white: '95 Sancerre, Chateau de Sancerre, Loire, France $$

MOOSE SUKIYAKI

Beef, venison, buffalo or pork can be substituted.

2 Tbsp.	vegetable oil	30 mL
1 1/2 lb.	boneless moose sirloin	750 g
3	garlic cloves, minced	3
1/2 c.	soy sauce	125 mL
3 Tbsp.	sugar	45 mL
3 Tbsp.	chicken broth	45 mL
1	large onion, thinly sliced	1
1	small green bell pepper, chopped	1
3/4 c.	thinly sliced celery	175 mL
1/2 lb.	fresh mushrooms, sliced	250 g
1	(8 fl. oz./227 mL) tin sliced bamboo shoots, drained	1
3/4 c.	sliced green onion	175 mL
1 Tbsp.	freshly grated ginger root	15 mL
1 Tbsp.	cornstarch, mixed with 2 Tbsp./30 mL chicken broth or water	15 mL

Heat oil in a large heavy skillet until very hot. Slice meat diagonally into strips; brown in batches in the hot oil. Blend together garlic, soy sauce, sugar and chicken broth; add half to meat in skillet; reduce heat to medium. Add onion, green bell pepper, celery and mushrooms; cover; reduce heat again and simmer 10 minutes.

Add remaining soy mixture to pan, together with the bamboo shoot slices. Simmer, uncovered, 4-5 minutes. Add green onion, simmer 1 minute. Add grated ginger and cornstarch mixture. Stir and cook until sauce thickens slightly.

MAKES: 4-6 servings

Serving suggestion: Serve over hot fluffy rice with a crunchy Caesar salad (see page 38).

Wine suggestion: Smooth, rich red: '95 Ruffino Chianti Classico riserva Ducale, Italy $$

British Columbia is a crucial part of the Pacific Flyway. Six million ducks pass through B.C. during the fall migration. Approximately one million ducks, plus a variety of other waterfowl such as snow geese and Canada geese, tundra and trumpeter swans winter in the province every year. In order to help protect these valuable resources, DU has located several offices in B.C. and is actively cooperating with local conservation groups, federal and provincial government departments, native bands and private landowners to improve habitat areas. To date, DUC has invested nearly $40 million in B.C. to reconstruct and maintain over 550 wetland areas.

BUFFALO SCALLOPINE WITH MUSHROOMS AND WHITE WINE

Beef or veal can be substituted.

1 1/4 lbs.	top sirloin buffalo, cut into 8-10 pieces	625 g
1/2 c.	flour	125 mL
	Salt and freshly ground black pepper	
2 Tbsp.	unsalted butter, divided	30 mL
2 Tbsp.	olive oil, divided	30 mL
1	medium onion, finely chopped	1
1 lb.	mushrooms, thinly sliced	500 g
1/2 c.	white wine	125 mL
1/2 c.	beef broth	125 mL
1 1/2 tsp.	minced fresh thyme	8 mL
2 Tbsp.	finely chopped parsley	30 mL

Place meat pieces between 2 pieces of waxed paper and with a meat tenderizer hammer or heavy utensil, pound the pieces into 1/8" (0.3 cm) thick scallops. Spread flour on a large piece of waxed paper; season with salt and pepper. Dredge scallops in the flour, coating evenly.

In a large skillet, heat 1 Tbsp. (15 mL) butter and 1 Tbsp. (15 mL) oil on medium-high, making sure the pan is hot. Slip scallops in batches into pan and sear them about 1 minute on each side. (Do not overcrowd the pan.) Transfer to a side plate; cover and keep warm.

Add remaining butter and oil to skillet; sauté onion for about 5-7 minutes on medium heat or until softened and lightly browned. Increase heat to high. Add mushrooms and continue sautéing, stirring occasionally, for about 5 more minutes or until the mushrooms are browned and have reclaimed their liquid. Add wine, broth and thyme to mushroom mixture; cook for about a minute on medium-high to reduce. Season to taste. Return scallops to skillet, turning to coat with sauce. Garnish with chopped parsley and serve immediately.

MAKES: 4 servings

Serving suggestion: Serve with egg noodles and crunchy snow peas.

Wine suggestion: Dense, complex red: '93 Errazuriz Don Maximiano Special Reserve, Chile $$

STEWED RABBIT WITH LENTILS

Chicken or Cornish game hen pieces can be substituted.

3/4 c.	dried red and green lentils	175 mL
2 Tbsp.	olive oil	30 mL
1	large rabbit, cleaned, cut-up	1
1	large onion, chunked	1
6	large garlic cloves, minced	6
$3^{1}/_{2}$ c.	tomato juice/V-8 juice	875 mL
	Grated peel of 1 lemon	
3/4 c.	packed fresh thyme leaves, minced	175 mL
1/2 tsp.	salt	3 mL
3/4 tsp.	coarse black pepper	4 mL
2 Tbsp.	Balsamic vinegar	30 mL

Place lentils in a medium bowl; cover with water. Let stand on counter overnight. When ready to start cooking, drain thoroughly, rinse and drain again.

Heat oil in a large Dutch oven until bubbly; add cleaned and dried rabbit pieces; cook pieces on both sides for about 2 minutes or until lightly browned. Remove pieces from pan. Add onion and garlic to pan; cook until onion is starting to soften (about 2-3 minutes), stirring frequently. Add lentils and tomato or V-8 juice, mixing well. Reduce heat to simmer; cover; cook about 1/2 hour. Add rabbit pieces, lemon peel, seasonings and vinegar; stir and replace lid. Simmer another 3/4 hour or until lentils are tender (stirring and turning rabbit once or twice during cooking).

MAKES: 3-4 servings

Serving suggestion: Serve with dumplings cooked on top for the last 20 minutes of cooking time.

Wine suggestion: Grapey red: '96 Père Anselme Côtes-du-Rhône, France $

Check out the Ducks Unlimited Canada website at www.ducks.ca (or the U.S. site for Ducks Unlimited Inc. at www.ducks.org). Choose from 6 different membership levels and give yourself the satisfaction of knowing that you are contributing to Canada's best known and most trusted conservation organization. For membership by phone, call 1-800-665-DUCK today!

BARBECUED ELK RIBS WITH CHIPOTLE MOLASSES BARBECUE SAUCE

Beef, lamb, pork ribs or chicken pieces can be substituted. This simple sauce accents the elk ribs beautifully. Chipotle chiles add a smooth smoky flavour. Make sure to brush the sauce on just before serving so the ribs stay brown and do not burn.

Sauce

1 Tbsp.	vegetable oil	15 mL
1	large onion, finely chopped	1
3	garlic cloves, minced	3
1	(5 1/2 fl. oz./156 mL) tin tomato paste	1
2 c.	apple cider	500 mL
1 Tbsp.	soy sauce	15 mL
2 Tbsp.	cider vinegar	30 mL
2 Tbsp.	molasses	30 mL
1/2 -1	Chipotle chile, finely chopped	1/2 -1
	Salt and pepper to taste	
3 lb.	elk ribs	1.5 kg

To make sauce: in a large saucepan heat oil on medium until hot. Add onion; cook about 5 minutes or until lightly browned. Add garlic; cook another minute. Add remaining ingredients and simmer on medium-low for about 15-20 minutes or until sauce is slightly thickened.

Prepare a barbecue, broiler or grill for medium-high cooking. Season ribs with salt and pepper; grill about 5 minutes on the meat side and 3-4 minutes on the rib side or until nicely browned. Brush continually with barbecue sauce and continue grilling about another minute on each side or until ribs are browned but not burnt. Serve ribs with remaining sauce (warm) on the side.

MAKES: 2 servings

NOTE: Make sure the extra sauce has not had contact with the meat.

Serving suggestion: Great with coleslaw and hot bread. Any remaining sauce (not having touched the ribs) can be refrigerated for use on other meats.

Wine suggestion: Ripe, dried-fruit red: '94 Masi Amarone Della Valpolicella Classico, Italy $$$

CAESAR SALAD WITH ROASTED CAPERS AND SEARED ELK TENDERLOIN

Beef, venison, buffalo, veal tenderloin or ostrich can be substituted. Beef will take longer to cook. Venison and veal less time.

1 lb.	elk tenderloin	500 g
1 Tbsp.	olive oil	15 mL
1 Tbsp.	lemon juice	15 mL
	Salt and freshly ground black pepper	
1/4 c.	drained, well rinsed large capers	60 mL
1 tsp.	olive oil	5 mL

Dressing

1	large egg	1
3	large garlic cloves, minced	3
1/4 c.	fresh lemon juice	60 mL
1-2 tsp.	anchovy paste (to taste)	5-10 mL
1/4 tsp.	black pepper	1 mL
1/2 c.	olive oil	125 mL
1/2 c.	freshly grated Asiago cheese , divided	125 mL
2	medium heads Romaine lettuce hearts, torn into bite-size pieces	

Place the tenderloin in a sealable plastic bag. Combine olive oil, lemon juice, salt and pepper; add to the meat; close bag. Roll the bag around a few times to make sure meat is well coated. Refrigerate 2-8 hours or overnight, turning once or twice.

Preheat oven to 400ºF. (200ºC). Place capers and the 1 tsp. (5 mL) oil in a small heavy roasting pan. Roast capers, turning a few times, for about 18-20 minutes or until crispy. Watch carefully towards the end. Remove from oven, drain and reserve.

Dressing: immerse egg in a small pan of boiling water. Remove pan from heat; cover for 10 minutes. Remove egg; let cool for 10 minutes. In a mini-chop, combine garlic, juice, anchovy paste and pepper. Crack the egg, spoon it into the mini chop. Pulse with other ingredients until combined. Add oil in a steady stream, with the motor running, until emulsified. Add 1/4 c. (60 mL) cheese. Taste for seasoning.

Prepare a broiler, barbecue or grill for medium-high heat. Remove meat from marinade; cook, about 4 minutes per side, for a total cooking time of 8-10 minutes. Make sure the interior is medium-rare. Slice thinly. In a large salad bowl combine lettuce and capers with the dressing; toss. Add remaining cheese; toss to coat. Place salad on cold plates; arrange filet slices on top. Serve immediately.

MAKES: 4-6 servings

Serving suggestion: Great with cheese-topped toasted baguette slices.

Wine suggestion: Rich, spicy red: '95 E & E Black Pepper Shiraz Barossa Valley, Australia $$$

SOUTHWESTERN-STYLE VENISON CHILI

Beef, buffalo or other mixtures of ground meat can be substituted.

6 Tbsp.	vegetable oil, divided	90 mL
3 lbs.	venison chuck, cut into 1/2" (1.25 cm) chunks	1.25 kg
3	large onions, finely chopped	3
1	Jalapeño chile, seeded, finely chopped	1
8	garlic cloves, minced	8
4 tsp.	ground oregano	20 mL
3 Tbsp.	ground cumin	45 mL
2 tsp.	ground coriander	10 mL
1 tsp.	ground cinnamon	5 mL
1/2 c.	chili powder or to taste	125 mL
1	can beer	1
2 1/2 c.	beef broth	625 mL
1	(28 fl. oz./796 mL) tin crushed tomatoes	1
1	Chipotle chile in adobo sauce, chopped	1
1 tsp.	salt	5 mL
1	*each* red and yellow bell peppers, seeded, cut into 1/2"(1.25 cm) dice	1
1	*each* (14 fl. oz./396 mL) tin kidney beans and pinto beans, drained	1
1/2 sq.	unsweetened chocolate, grated	1/2
	Salt and freshly ground black pepper	

In a large, 6-qt. (6 L) pot, heat 2 Tbsp. (30 mL) oil over medium heat. Cook meat in batches until it is well-browned on all sides, about 5-7 minutes. (Don't crowd the pan or the meat will steam.) Remove chunks; reserve as you cook.

Add another 2 Tbsp. (30 mL) oil; cook onions until soft and lightly browned, about 5-7 minutes. Add Jalapeño chile; cook another minute. Add garlic, oregano, cumin, coriander, cinnamon and chili powder; cook another 2 minutes or until the spices have mixed together, stirring constantly.

Add beer, broth, tomatoes, chipotle chile and salt; bring to a low simmer. Return meat to the pot. Simmer, partially covered, 1 1/2 hours, stirring occasionally.

Add bell peppers, kidney and pinto beans to the chili mixture on medium heat, uncovered, and continue simmering for 10 more minutes or until slightly thickened. (If the mixture thickens too much just add a bit of broth or water.)

Add grated chocolate; stir until melted. Taste and add salt and pepper if needed.

MAKES: 3 qt. (3 L) or 8-10 servings

Serving suggestion: Serve in large chili bowls surrounded by small bowls of sour cream, salsa, grated Cheddar cheese and chopped onions.

Wine suggestion: Spicy, round red: '96 Bodegas Palacio "Cosme Palacio y Hermanos" Tinto, Spain $$

STIR-FRIED VENISON WITH EGGPLANT AND GREEN ONIONS

Beef or lamb can be substituted for the venison.

Marinade

1	egg white	1
2 Tbsp.	soy sauce	30 mL
1 Tbsp.	cornstarch	15 mL
1 lb.	boneless leg of venison (or sirloin or flank steak) cut into 2"x 1/2"(5 x 1.25 cm) strips	500 g

Sauce

3 Tbsp.	*each* rice wine vinegar and hoisin sauce	45 mL
1 Tbsp.	chili paste with garlic	15 mL
1 tsp.	dark sesame oil, or to taste	5 mL
3 Tbsp.	chicken or beef broth or water	45 mL
3 Tbsp.	peanut oil, divided	45 mL
4	Japanese eggplants, cut into 2"x 1/2" (5 x 1.25 cm) strips	4
4	green onions, cut into 1" (2.5 cm) pieces on the diagonal	4

Marinade: whisk egg white, soy sauce and cornstarch together in a medium bowl. Add meat; toss to coat; marinate for up to 4 hours in the refrigerator.

Sauce: in a small bowl, place all 5 ingredients; stir to combine. Set aside.

In a wok over high heat, add 2 Tbsp. (30 mL) oil, swirling to coat the sides. When oil is very hot but not smoking, add eggplant; toss every 15-20 seconds for 3-4 minutes or until eggplant is slightly softened. Briefly toss green onions in the wok with eggplant for a minute; transfer to a bowl and reserve.

Add remaining oil to wok on high heat. When oil is very hot but not smoking; add half the meat; toss every 15-20 seconds for 3-4 minutes or until brown. Add more oil, if needed; repeat with remaining meat. Return eggplant and green onions to wok with meat and add sauce. Cook for 2 more minutes, stirring to evenly coat ingredients. Serve immediately.

MAKES: 4 servings

Serving suggestion: Serve with steamed white rice. You can also add a julienned red or yellow bell pepper for extra colour, if desired.

Wine suggestion: Peppery red: '95 Delas Frères "Les Launes" Crozes Hermitage, France $$

BUFFALO TOURTIERE

Beef, veal, pork, venison or a combination of meats can be substituted.

	Pastry for a 9" (23 cm) double crust pie	
1/2 lb.	ground buffalo	250 g
1/2 lb.	ground pork	250 g
1	medium onion, diced	1
3	large garlic cloves, minced	3
1	(10 fl. oz./284 mL) tin beef broth	1
1/2 tsp.	salt	3 mL
1/2 tsp.	coarse black pepper	3 mL
1/2 tsp.	ground sage	3 mL
1/2 tsp.	ground mace	3 mL
1/4 tsp.	ground cloves	2 mL
1 Tbsp.	minced fresh thyme	15 mL
3/4 c.	instant mashed potato flakes	175 mL
1	egg, beaten	1

Preheat oven to 425ºF. (220ºC). Roll out half of the pastry on a floured board to a circle about 12" (27.5 cm) in diameter. Fit into the pie plate, taking care not to stretch the dough. Press into the bottom and sides, leaving the extra hanging over the edge. Place in the refrigerator along with the other half of the pastry while you make the filling.

In a medium saucepan, combine all remaining ingredients except the beaten egg. Cook, uncovered, over medium-high heat until thickened and all pink has disappeared from the meat and all liquid has been absorbed. Place in front of a fan or in the refrigerator until cool. Spread evenly in the cold pie shell. Roll out remaining half of pastry to another large circle. Make two slits in the middle. Lift onto the pie; roll outer edges of both top and bottom crust together to make a secure seal; flute decoratively. Brush pastry with beaten egg.

Bake about 20-30 minutes or until pastry is well-browned.

MAKES: 6 servings

Serving suggestion: Serve in wedges with mimosa salad, Dijon mustard and crusty bread.

Wine suggestion: Rich, strong red: '95 Ridge Vineyards Petit Syrah, Geyserville, California $$$

NOTE: Tourtière is also good cold with salad for picnics.

GAME

ELK OSSO BUCCO

Beef, veal or venison can be substituted.

4 Tbsp.	olive oil, divided	60 mL
6	large, meaty elk shanks, cut 2"(5cm) thick	6
	Salt and freshly ground black pepper	
2	large onions, finely chopped	2
3	large carrots, peeled, finely chopped	3
3	large celery stalks, finely chopped	3
4	garlic cloves, minced	4
2	medium yams, peeled, cut into small dice, about 2 c. (500 mL)	2
1 c.	white wine	250 mL
2	(14 fl. oz./398 mL) tins diced plum tomatoes with juice	2
1¹/2 c.	beef or chicken broth	375 mL
1	piece orange peel	1
1	piece lemon peel	1
1 tsp.	chopped fresh thyme leaves (or 1/4 tsp./1 mL) dried	5 mL
1	bay leaf	1
1/4 c.	finely chopped fresh parsley, divided	60 mL
2 tsp.	finely chopped lemon peel	10 mL

In a large skillet heat 2 Tbsp. (30 mL) oil on medium-high. Season shanks with salt and pepper; brown in batches, about 4 minutes per side. Remove and reserve. (You can also broil, barbecue or grill the shanks over medium-high heat about 4 minutes per side.)

Preheat oven to 325ºF. (160ºC). In a large, non-stick heavy casserole that will hold the shanks in a single layer, heat remaining oil on medium. Add onion, carrots and celery; cook, stirring often, until vegetables are softened, about 5-8 minutes. Add garlic; cook 1 minute. Add yams; cook 1 minute.

Increase to high; add wine; cook until most of the liquid has been reduced, about 2 minutes. Add tomatoes, broth, peel pieces, thyme and bay leaf. Place the reserved shanks in a single layer in the pan, bring to a boil; cover; bake for about 2 hours for elk or 1 1/2 hours for veal or until the meat is very tender. (Some of the shanks may cook faster than others; make sure they are all tender before serving.) Remove bay leaf and peel pieces. Stir in 2 Tbsp. (30 mL) parsley. Garnish with remaining parsley and lemon peel; serve.

MAKES: 4-6 servings

Serving suggestion: Excellent with pasta and salad.

Wine suggestion: Cedary smooth red: '95 Château d'Angludet, Bordeaux, France $$$

VENISON MEDALLIONS WITH PORT MUSHROOM SAUCE

Beef, veal, pork or buffalo can be substituted.

Sauce

1 oz.	dried chopped Porcini, Morels or Shiitake mushrooms	30 g
2 Tbsp.	unsalted butter	30 mL
2	medium leeks, cleaned, finely chopped	2
1/2 lb.	*each* brown and Shiitake mushrooms, sliced	250 g
1/4 c.	tawny port	60 mL
1/2 c.	beef or veal broth	125 mL
1/4 c.	whipping cream	60 mL
	Salt and freshly ground black pepper	
2 Tbsp.	canola oil	30 mL
1	boneless loin of venison (about 1 1/2 lbs. /750 g), cut into 8-3 oz. (90 g) medallions	1
2 Tbsp.	finely chopped parsley	30 mL

Place dried mushrooms in a medium saucepan; cover with water; bring to a boil. Remove from heat; let stand 1/2 hour. Strain mushrooms through a fine-meshed sieve, reserving liquid. Set mushrooms and liquid aside.

In a large skillet, melt butter on medium-high. Sauté leeks 5-7 minutes or until softened and lightly browned. Add fresh brown and Shiitake mushrooms; sauté, stirring occasionally, until softened, about 3-5 minutes. Add port, broth, 1/2 c. (125 mL) reserved mushroom liquid and reserved soaked mushrooms; reduce for about 3 minutes. Add cream; simmer 2-3 minutes or until it is a sauce-like consistency. Add salt and pepper to taste. Reserve.

Heat oil in a large sauté pan. Season medallions with salt and pepper. When the pan is very hot, sear medallions, in batches, for about 2 minutes on one side and 1 minute on the other. Make sure the medallions are medium-rare.

MAKES: 4 servings

Serving suggestion: Spoon about 1/2 c. (125 mL) mushroom sauce on each serving plate, mounding the mushrooms in the center. Arrange two medallions on top and garnish with chopped parsley.

Wine suggestion: Powerful red: '94 Arrowhead Sonoma County Cabernet Sauvignon, California $$$

BUFFALO CARPACCIO on TOMATO BOCCONCINI and BASIL SALAD

Beef, veal, ostrich, duck or venison carpaccio can be substituted.

1	piece buffalo loin (about 2-2 1/2 lb./ 1 kg)	1
2 Tbsp.	extra virgin olive oil	30 mL
1 Tbsp.	Balsamic vinegar	15 mL
2 Tbsp.	crushed pink, green and black peppercorns	30 mL
1 Tbsp.	minced fresh garlic	15 mL
1 Tbsp.	dried basil	15 mL
4 Tbsp.	Balsamic vinegar	60 mL
1-2 Tbsp.	grainy Dijon mustard	15-30 mL
1/2 tsp.	coarse black pepper	3 mL
3/4 tsp.	salt	4 mL
3 Tbsp.	pine nuts	45 mL
1 c.	firmly packed fresh basil leaves	250 mL
5 Tbsp.	extra virgin olive oil	75 mL
4	large ripe tomatoes, thickly sliced	4
4	large fresh Bocconcini balls, thickly sliced *	4
	Whole fresh basil leaves	

**Bocconcini is fresh Mozzarella - usually sold in deli departments.*

Make sure the loin is the same thickness along its length so it cooks evenly. Trim any visible fat. Combine next 5 ingredients in a small bowl; mix well. Rub all over meat, pressing on firmly. Cover; refrigerate in a non-metallic dish in refrigerator up to 2 days. When ready to cook, preheat oven to 450° F. (230℃). Roast 15 minutes until outside is browned but the inside is still raw. Let cool completely; wrap in plastic wrap; place in freezer until very firm but not frozen.

Meanwhile, combine next 7 ingredients in a food processor or bowl with a hand-held blender. Process until smooth; place in a large bowl with the tomato and Bocconcini slices. Toss to coat completely. Refrigerate if necessary until meat is firm.

Remove meat from freezer; using a very sharp unserrated knife (or a meat slicer) slice as thinly as possible. (You can also take it to your local butcher for a more professional job.) Arrange marinated tomato and cheese slices on four cold dinner plates. Top with swirls of carpaccio; toss whole basil leaves over top.

MAKES: 4 servings (Leftover meat can be kept in the freezer for later use. Thaw slightly and slice.)

Serving suggestion: Serve with cracked black pepper over top.

Wine suggestion: Earthy red: '95 Antonin Rodet Château de Chamirey, France $$$

VENISON STEW with DRIED FRUIT

Beef, lamb or pork can be substituted.

2 lb.	boneless venison	1 kg
1/3 c.	flour	75 mL
1/4 c.	olive oil, divided	60 mL
2	onions, chopped	2
3	garlic cloves, minced	3
3	carrots, cut into 1"(2.5 cm) cubes	3
$2\frac{1}{2}$ lb.	rutabaga, cut into 1"(2.5 cm) cubes	1 kg
1	(19 fl. oz. /397 mL) tin plum tomatoes, undrained, chopped	1
2 Tbsp.	red wine vinegar	30 mL
2	bay leaves	2
2 tsp.	minced fresh ginger	10 mL
1 tsp.	*each* ground cinnamon, coriander and cumin	5 mL
1/2 tsp.	*each* fennel seeds, salt and pepper	3 mL
$2\frac{1}{2}$ c.	beef broth	625 mL
2 Tbsp.	liquid honey	30 mL
1/2 c.	*each* dried apricots and pitted prunes	125 mL
1/2 c.	halved dried figs	125 mL
1/4 c.	chopped fresh parsley	60 mL

Cut meat into 1"(2.5 cm) cubes; toss with flour. In large heavy Dutch oven, heat 2 Tbsp. (30 mL) oil over medium-high; brown meat in batches, adding remaining oil as needed. Remove to bowl; set aside.

Add onions and garlic to Dutch oven; cook 5 minutes or until softened. Stir in carrots, rutabaga, tomatoes and their liquid, vinegar, bay leaves, ginger, cinnamon, coriander, cumin, fennel seeds, salt, pepper, broth, honey and meat with any accumulated juices. Bring to boil, scraping up browned bits on bottom of pan. Return heat to medium-low; cover pan; simmer 2 hours, stirring occasionally. Add apricots, prunes and figs; simmer, uncovered, 45 minutes or until meat is tender. Remove bay leaves; taste and adjust seasoning. Sprinkle parsley over top. (Stew can be cooled, covered and refrigerated for up to 2 days or frozen for up to 1 month.)

MAKES: 4-6 servings

Serving suggestion: Add crusty bread and a crisp coleslaw.

Wine suggestion: Big plummy red: '93 Castello Banfi Brunello di Montalcino, Italy $$$

GAME

VENISON SAUSAGES PUTTANESCA

Lamb, pork, beef or any combination meat highly-flavoured sausages can be substituted.

8	large venison sausages	8
3	garlic cloves, minced	3
1 doz.	shallots, peeled, halved	1 doz
1	red or green Jalapeño chile, seeded, minced	1
1	(14 fl. oz./398 mL) tin chopped plum tomatoes	1
1	170 g tin whole black olives, drained, halved	1
2 Tbsp.	drained capers	30 mL
3 Tbsp.	chopped fresh basil	45 mL
1/2 tsp.	coarse black pepper	3 mL
	Coarse pickling salt (optional)	

Heat a large skillet; add sausages and cook on all sides until browned. Remove and keep warm. Pour off all but 2 Tbsp (30 mL) fat from the pan. Add garlic and shallots. Cook and stir occasionally until browned and starting to soften. Add Jalapeño, tomatoes, olives and capers. Keep heat high and cook, stirring occasionally, until sauce starts to thicken. Add sausages to pan for 1 minute. Add basil and pepper, cooking 1 minute more. Mixture should still be "saucy" but not liquid.

MAKES: 4 servings

Serving suggestion: Serve at once on hot plates with a green vegetable and bulgar wheat or couscous. Sprinkle with the pickling salt if desired.

Wine suggestion: Dense, curranty red: '90 Raimat Cabernet Sauvignon, Spain $$

Alberta is home to 20% of all the ducks surveyed each spring in North America. Poor nest success as a result of intensive farming has severely reduced the quantity and quality of grassland nest cover, making nests easier for predators to find. A recent DUC initiative in conjunction with partners in Alberta Forestry, Lands and Wildlife is called Alberta Prairie Care (APC) and is dedicated to improving much-needed upland nesting cover in the critical waterfowl production areas of the province.

RABBIT QUESADILLAS
WITH CARAMELIZED ONIONS
AND JACK CHEESE

Cooked chicken or turkey can be substituted. You can prepare the filling the day before and then assemble quesadillas before serving.

1	(2 lb./1 kg) rabbit, cut into pieces, poached 20 minutes in boiling salted water	1
1 Tbsp.	vegetable oil	15 mL
2	large red onions, thinly sliced	2
1/2 c.	beer	125 mL
2 Tbsp.	Balsamic vinegar	30 mL
1 tsp.	sugar	5 mL
1	medium Jalapeño chile, seeded, finely chopped	1
1 tsp.	finely chopped fresh oregano or 1/2 tsp. (3 mL) dried	5 mL
	Salt and pepper	
3	large (12"/30 cm) flour tortillas	3
1 1/2 c.	shredded Monterey Jack cheese	375 mL
	Guacamole	
	Salsa	
	Sour cream	

Cool rabbit in stock. Drain rabbit; shred meat into bite-sized slices. (This should be about 1 1/2 c./375 mL.) Reserve.

Heat oil in a large non-aluminum casserole on medium-high. Add onions; cook for about 10-15 minutes or until golden brown and well softened, stirring frequently. Add beer, Balsamic vinegar, sugar and Jalapeño to onions; simmer on low heat until almost all the liquid has evaporated. The onions should be very tender and slightly caramelized. Add oregano, salt and pepper; taste for seasoning; cool.

Lightly grease or spray a 12"/30 cm non-stick skillet or griddle; place on medium-high. Place a tortilla in skillet and spoon 1/2 c. (125 mL) of onion mixture evenly on the bottom half of the tortilla. Sprinkle with about 1/3 of shredded rabbit mixture and top evenly with 1/2 c. (125 mL) shredded cheese; fold over tortilla in half pressing down with a spatula. Cook quesadilla until lightly brown; turn over and cook other side until lightly brown. Place on a cutting board; cut into triangles; keep warm by covering with foil. Repeat steps to cook remaining quesadillas.

MAKES: 6 appetizers or 3 entrées.

Serving suggestion: Arrange on a large serving platter with guacamole, salsa and/or sour cream.

Wine suggestion: Crisp, off-dry white: '95 Selbach Detzemer Maximer Klosterlay Riesling Spätlese, Germany $

FISH

F!SH

LIFE UNDER THE WATER

In the wetlands protected by Ducks Unlimited are creatures that have changed little since prehistoric times; fish, reptiles and amphibians. Amphibians have been with us for more than 410 million years. They were the first vertebrates to climb onto land. From them came reptiles, which were followed by birds and mammals. Including us.

Turtles, semi-aquatic marsh dwellers, can trace their family tree for 200 million years. Turtles hobnobbed with dinosaurs. There was a turtle thought to have known Napoleon during Bonaparte's 1815-21 exile on St. Helena. A century later, a New York historian believed the turtle was still alive, and applied for a grant to travel to the South Atlantic island to interview the carapaced crawler.

Many fish also enjoy long lives. Carp and eels can swim contentedly for 50 years, and even a goldfish has been known to reach 40. A gigantic sturgeon caught in Ontario's Lake of the Woods in 1953 was thought to be 150 years old, but this may be just another fish story.

There are ways to estimate the age of fish, and Gary Carder knows them all. Carder spent more than a quarter-century with Canada's Department of Fisheries and Oceans, most of it in the Northwest Territories and British Columbia. By checking the age and size of fish, he was able to keep track of the sea's inventory. "If fish are getting younger and smaller," he says, "we've got a problem."

Among the ways to gauge a fish's age is to count the rings in its ears. "There's an aging structure in fish ears called an otolith," says Carder. "To determine a fish's age this way is like counting rings on trees." With other species, age is determined by scales, dorsal fins and other features. Could a sturgeon be 150 years old? Gary Carder knows that these gigantic caviar carriers can live more than a century.

The most interesting fish for Carder, however, is the Arctic char. "I've worked with them for 25 years," he says, "and as time goes by, I find their life history more and more complex."

Wetlands are breeding grounds for all sorts of finned, furry and flying creatures, including pike, eel, carp, perch, frogs, toads, snails, clams, crayfish, muskrats, beavers, otters, dragonflies, crane flies and mosquitoes. Many lay eggs in the water. In coastal streams, trout and salmon co-exist. Anchovies and mullet reside in salt marshes. Florida's mangrove swamps are home to tarpon and grey snapper. In these same tropical areas between Ten Thousand Islands and Florida Bay live ospreys, egrets, cormorants, cuckoos, spoonbills, lobster, shrimp and snapper – about 450 species of fish, reptiles, amphibians, mammals and birds.

The near miraculous migratory patterns of some fish are well known. Thousands of people travel to the Adams River in British Columbia's Shuswap country to watch the arrival of Pacific Ocean salmon that have battled against currents and virtually flown up waterfalls to their ancient, familial breeding waters. But salmon aren't the only fish that travel thousands of miles to spawn. American eels leave their fresh water homes in North American streams to spawn near the West Indies. Herring journey from the North Sea between Denmark and Norway to spawn off the coast of England.

Water temperature, geographic features and odours are guides to the fish. Odours are important in other ways. Yellow bullhead identify each other through scent, and cichlids recognize their young by odour. There are fear scents among fish, just as there are among humans and other animals, and – again like humans – fish are attracted to each other sexually through pheromones, hormonal secretions that have a near irresistible impact on the olfactory sense.

LURES AND LORE

*"The only reason I ever played golf
was so I could afford to hunt and fish."* – Sam Snead

There are many legends involving fish, especially among the First Nations of Canada's Pacific coast. There is, for example, the salmon that turns itself into copper. To the Kwakiutl people, the toad was also a bringer of copper. A legendary hero to the Katzie people was Swaneset, who climbed a ladder of arrows to worship the Lord Who Dwells Above, and ended by marrying the Lord's daughter. Her dowry: the sockeye salmon.

In another version of this story, Swaneset marries the Princess of the Sockeye Salmon People. "We are different from all other beings," she tells him. "Part of the year we are human beings, but at a certain season, we change into salmon and travel in the sea." When the Salmon Wife bears Swaneset's son, British Columbia's Fraser River is filled with sockeye.

This brings to mind the mermaid, whose name comes from the French "mer" (sea). The mermaid, with the beauteous head and torso of a maiden but the tail of a fish, has been known since the fourteenth century. About 200 years later, a merman also surfaced, but never exerted the same fascination as his female counterpart (although nostalgia buffs may remember an Action Comics superhero of the 1930s named Submariner, who had pointed ears like Mr. Spock's and traveled underwater). Interestingly, the egg cases of the skate, ray and shark are called mermaid's purses.

The prehistoric sea monster is present in many cultures. The best known of these creatures are Scotland's Loch Ness monster and British Columbia's Ogopogo. Massive monetary rewards have been offered to anyone able to prove the existence of these denizens of the deep, but no one has been able to snare, land or convincingly photograph either one.

Fish turn up in numerous, usually unflattering, expressions, such as "queer fish," "poor fish," "fish out of water" and "drinks like a fish." Despite this last phrase, there are no 12-step programs for fish.

There are some 22,000 species of fish, divided into various categories. Pisces (Latin for "fish" and the twelfth sign of the Zodiac) is the best known of these, but this classification refers only to fish with jaws.

The artistry in the development of fishermen's lures or flies is widely acknowledged and there have been exhibitions of flies in art museums, as duck decoys are now recognized as examples of the carver's art.

The fish was also an early symbol – a code – of Christianity. The Greek word ichthus (fish) formed an acronym of the key letters in Jesus Christ, Son of God, Savior. The fish symbol can be seen still on the bumper stickers of church campers.

GREAT FISH STORIES

Almost as well known in storytelling as the words "once upon a time" is the phrase "the one that got away." The most famous stories of sea creatures involve whales: the tale of Jonah ("he made his home in/that fish's abdomen") and "Moby Dick," which may not be whoppers, but are certainly about whoppers. In both stories, the marine mammal gets away. It's hard to land a metaphor.

There have always been great writers on wildlife – on nature, hunting, fishing, wilderness treks. The first classic book on fishing was "The Compleat Angler," written by Izaak Walton in 1653. It is, wrote Kenneth Rexroth in "Classics Revisited," "bathed in a light that comes from a lucid heart." A small contemporary masterpiece is "The Spawning Run" by William Humphries, an account of salmon fishing in Scotland.

And there are other great fish stories – but none so well remembered as two by Ernest Hemingway: his 1952 novella "The Old Man and the Sea," the last stroke needed to bring him the Nobel Prize for Literature, and "Big Two-Hearted River," a two-part story from 1924 based on a trout fishing expedition Hemingway took in 1919 in the woods of upper Michigan, on the peninsula nicknamed "the thumb." Like so much of Hemingway's writing, it leads to the discovery of spiritual peace: "He felt he had left everything behind him, the need for thinking, the need to write, other needs. It was all back of him. [Now] He had made his camp. He was settled. Nothing could touch him. He was there, in the good place. He was in his home where he had made it."

PAPIOTTE OF ARCTIC CHAR

Any salmon or trout can be substituted.

4	pieces parchment paper, *each 12" x 8" (30 x 20 cm)*	4
2	small carrots	2
1	stalk celery	1
1	small leek, white portion only	1
1	red bell pepper	1
4	skinned Arctic Char fillets (each 4 oz./125 g)	4
2 Tbsp.	dry white wine	30 mL
2 Tbsp.	lemon or lime juice	30 mL
2 Tbsp.	unsalted butter, melted	30 mL
	Pinch salt and pepper	
4	lemon or lime slices	4
	Sprigs fresh basil, chervil, coriander or tarragon	
	Vegetable oil	

Preheat oven to 400ºF.(200ºC). Cut parchment paper into heart-shaped pieces, using the full width of the paper. Set aside.

Cut carrots, celery, leeks and bell pepper into very thin julienne strips. Blanch vegetable strips in boiling water for about 2 minutes or until tender-crisp. Cool in bowl of ice water; drain.

Place fillets on right side of each heart. Divide vegetables into 4 portions and place a portion on top of each fillet. Sprinkle wine and lemon juice on top. Drizzle melted butter and sprinkle pinch salt and pepper on top. Place lemon slice and a couple of sprigs of herbs on top.

Fold left side of heart over fillet; tightly seal packet by making a series of tight, over-lapping folds along the edge. Lightly brush each heart with oil. Place packets on a baking sheet and bake for 10 minutes or until packets are puffed and lightly browned. Cooking time will depend on thickness of the fish.

MAKES: 4 servings

Serving suggestion: Excellent with potatoes au gratin and a crisp green vegetable.

Wine suggestion: Fruity white: '96 Seaview Chardonnay, Australia $

RED SNAPPER VERRACRUZ

Cod, sea bass, orange roughy, Petrale sole or halibut can be substituted for the red snapper.

1 1/3 lbs.	red snapper fillets	675 g
3 Tbsp.	fresh lime juice	45 mL
1/2 tsp.	salt	3 mL
1 Tbsp.	olive oil	15 mL
1/2	medium onion, sliced very thinly	1/2
2	garlic cloves, minced	2
1	Jalapeño pepper, seeded, finely chopped	1
4	Roma tomatoes, cut in quarters	4
12	pimento-stuffed green olives	12
2 Tbsp.	chopped fresh cilantro	30 mL

Place fish fillets in a flat non-metallic dish; brush with lime juice; sprinkle with salt; cover; marinate at room temperature for 2 hours, turning several times. Drain; discard marinade.

Preheat oven to 450ºF.(230ºC). In a medium skillet, heat olive oil; add onion; cook over medium heat until onion is transparent. Add garlic, Jalapeño, tomatoes, olives and cilantro; simmer, uncovered, for 13-15 minutes, until tomatoes are cooked and sauce is thick.

Place drained fillets in a single layer in a shallow baker; pour sauce over. Bake, uncovered, for 10-15 minutes, until fish is opaque. Cooking time will vary with thickness of the fish. Allow about 10 minutes per 1" (2.5cm) thickness.

MAKES: 4 servings

Serving suggestion: Add a pilaf and fresh frenched beans.

Wine suggestion: Smooth, peppery red: '96 Paul Jaboulet Parallèle 45 Côtes-du-Rhône, France $

NASI GORENG

3 c.	water	750 mL
1 1/2 c.	long grain white rice	375 mL
1/4 c.	peanut oil, divided	60 mL
3	small carrots, peeled, diced	3
1/2 lb.	mushrooms, cleaned, diced	250 g
1	red bell pepper, seeded, diced	1
1 lb.	peeled, deveined raw prawns *or* shrimp	500 g
3	*each* green onions and shallots, finely chopped	3
3	garlic cloves, minced	3
1 Tbsp.	minced fresh ginger	15 mL
2	small green or red hot chiles, seeded, finely chopped	2
1 tsp.	paprika	5 mL
2 Tbsp.	ketchup	30 mL
2 Tbsp.	soy sauce	30 mL
1/4 lb.	fresh bean sprouts (about 2 c./500 mL)	125 g
	Chopped English cucumber	
	Peanuts	

In a large saucepan with a lid, heat water on medium-high until boiling. Add rice; turn down heat to medium-low; cover; simmer for about 20 minutes or until rice is cooked and water is absorbed. Remove from heat; transfer rice to a large baking sheet to cool, separating any clumps. This can be done up to 8 hours ahead and no less than 3 hours before stir-frying. Be sure to have the rice cooled to room temperature for the best result.

Heat 2 Tbsp. (30 mL) oil in a large wok or skillet on high heat. When oil is hot and almost smoking, add carrots, mushrooms and red bell pepper; stir-fry for about 1 minute or until slightly softened. Add prawns and green onion; toss every 15-20 seconds for 1 minute or until prawns just turn pink. Remove vegetables and prawns to a side bowl and reserve.

Add remaining 2 Tbsp. (30 mL) oil to wok or skillet. When very hot and almost smoking, stir-fry shallots for about 1 minute or until lightly browned. Add garlic, ginger and chiles; toss for about 30 seconds.

Add rice, spreading evenly around wok or skillet. Let cook about 10 seconds; toss to combine and coat ingredients. Add paprika, ketchup and soy sauce; toss to blend. Add reserved vegetables and shrimp; toss again, making sure to evenly distribute ingredients. Add bean sprouts and toss once more. Taste for seasoning. Transfer to a large serving bowl or platter and garnish with chopped cucumber and peanuts. Serve immediately.

MAKES: 4 servings

Serving suggestion: Serve with a cold snap pea salad.

Wine suggestion: Crisp, honeyed: '96 Hogue Chenin Blanc, Washington $

ORANGE ROUGHY WITH ORANGE-CHIVE SAUCE

Thick sole, thin snapper or catfish fillets can be substituted. Cooking time will vary. This refreshing citrus sauce complements the delicate orange roughy. This is a great standby for a last minute in-a-hurry meal.

1 Tbsp.	fresh orange juice	15 mL
1 tsp.	grated orange peel	5 mL
2	medium garlic cloves, minced	2
1 Tbsp.	finely chopped chives	15 mL
1/2 c.	mayonnaise	125 mL
2 Tbsp.	plain yoghurt	30 mL
4	orange roughy fillets, skinned, 1/3-1/2 lb. (165-250 g) each	4
2 Tbsp.	chopped chives	30 mL

In a small bowl combine first 6 ingredients; mix well.

Preheat broiler. Place fillets upside down on a sprayed broiler pan; spread 1 Tbsp. (15 mL) sauce on top of the fish. Broil fish about 3"(7.5 cm) from heat for 2 minutes or until nicely browned. Turn fish over carefully with a spatula and spread with remaining sauce. Return fish to broiler; broil until bubbly and well browned. Be careful not to let it burn. Using a large spatula, remove fish from broiler pan, taking care not to break the pieces. Place fish on hot plates; garnish with chives.

MAKES: 4 servings

Serving suggestion: Serve with a simple rice pilaf and steamed asparagus.

Wine suggestion: Creamy, crisp bubbly: Piper Heidsick Brut Champagne, France $$$

CAJUN TROUT WITH SOUR CREAM AND CUCUMBER SAUCE

Any trout, small salmon or Arctic char can be substituted.

Sour Cream Sauce

1/2 c.	light sour cream	125 mL
1/4 c.	light mayonnaise	60 mL
2 tsp.	Dijon mustard	10 mL
1/4 c.	chopped fresh chives	60 mL
1/4 c.	chopped fresh dill	60 mL
1/4 c.	grated English cucumber (peel on)	60 mL
2 tsp.	lemon juice	10 mL
	Salt and pepper	

Cajun Fish

2 tsp.	paprika	10 mL
1/2 tsp.	*each* salt, pepper, chili powder and dry mustard	3 mL
1/4 tsp.	*each* dried oregano and thyme	2 mL
	Pinch cayenne	
1 lb.	Cutthroat trout fillets	500 g
1 Tbsp.	olive oil	15 mL
1/4 c.	chopped fresh chives	60 mL
	Lime wedges	

Sour Cream Sauce: in a bowl, combine all ingredients; set aside.

Cajun Fish: preheat broiler. In small bowl, combine paprika, salt, pepper, chili powder, dry mustard, oregano, thyme and cayenne; set aside.

Pat fillets dry; lightly brush both sides of fillets with oil. Sprinkle spice mixture over both sides of fillets; place on greased or foil-lined broiler pan, skin side down.

Broil 4-6" (10-15 cm) from heat. Broil 4-5 minutes or until fish flakes easily with a fork. Sprinkle chives on top.

MAKES: 4 servings

Serving suggestion: Serve with Sour Cream Sauce and lime wedges along with double-baked potatoes and a green vegetable.

Wine suggestion: Fruity red: '95 Berberana Tempranillo Dragon Label, Spain $

CURRIED RED SNAPPER

Cod, Petrale sole, bass, orange roughy or catfish can be substituted. Cooking times will vary with the thickness of the fish.

1 Tbsp.	butter or margarine	15 mL
1 tsp.	vegetable oil	5 mL
1	large onion, finely chopped	1
2	garlic cloves, minced	2
1"	piece fresh ginger, peeled and slivered	2.5 cm
2 tsp.	curry powder or to taste	10 mL
3/4 c.	tomato sauce	175 mL
2	medium tomatoes, peeled, seeded and diced	2
	Salt, to taste	
1 1/3 lbs.	red snapper fillets	675 g
	Cooked rice	

In a large skillet, heat butter and oil until bubbly; add onion; cook over medium-low heat for 6 minutes, until onion is soft but not brown.

Add garlic, ginger and curry powder; cook 1 minute; add tomato sauce, diced tomatoes and salt; stir to mix.

Lay fish fillets in a single layer on top of sauce; spoon some sauce over; cover skillet; simmer 7-8 minutes, until fish is opaque and flakes easily with a fork.

MAKES: 4 servings

Serving suggestion: Serve on top of rice with a green vegetable of your choice.

Wine suggestion: Round, citrusy white: '94 Wente Riva Ranch Chardonnay, California $$

Among the 600 species benefitting from habitat conservation work by Ducks Unlimited are the Lazuli bunting, the Inca dove, the Chihuahuan raven, the Montezuma quail, the Nashville warbler, the yellow-breasted chat, the black-bellied whistling duck, the laughing gull, the brown booby, the American avocet, the California leaf-nosed bat, the Barren Ground caribou, the Siskiyou chipmunk and the Hoary marmot.

NEW ENGLAND CLAM CHOWDER

3 lbs.	clams in their shells, well cleaned	1.5 kg
1 c.	clam nectar or fish broth	250 mL
2 Tbsp.	unsalted butter	30 mL
1	onion, finely chopped	1
1/2 c.	diced salt pork	125 mL
2	carrots, peeled and thinly sliced	2
1	stalk celery, thinly sliced	1
1	small red or yellow bell pepper, diced	1
2 Tbsp.	flour	30 mL
2	medium waxy red or white potatoes, diced	2
3 c.	homogenized milk or half and half	750 mL
1	bay leaf	1
	Salt and freshly ground white pepper	
2 Tbsp.	finely chopped fresh parsley	30 mL
2 Tbsp.	chopped mixed fresh herbs	30 mL

Place clams in a large saucepan with broth; bring to a boil on medium-high. Reduce heat to simmer; steam clams until they open, about 5 minutes. Remove from heat; discard any clams that have not opened. Remove clams from their shells (cut in half if very large).

Strain clam juice through a fine sieve lined with cheesecloth. Reserve. (You should have about 1 1/2-2 c./375-500 mL.)

Melt butter in a 4 qt. (4 L) pan on medium; sauté onion until softened, about 3-5 minutes. Add salt pork; sauté another 2 minutes or until pork is cooked through, stirring occasionally. Add carrot, celery and bell pepper; sauté another minute. Add flour; cook for another 2 minutes, stirring to cook flour. Add strained clam juice, diced potatoes, milk and bay leaf; bring to a simmer on medium-high. Cook for about 15 minutes or until potatoes are tender. Remove bay leaf; season with salt and pepper; add parsley, herbs and shucked clams. Cook another minute to warm clams. Can be made ahead and refrigerated.

MAKES: 4 servings

Serving suggestion: Serve with little crackers or croûtons in heated bowls with bread sticks and salad.

Wine suggestion: Zippy white: Zomin Frizzante Pinot Chardonnay, Italy $

POBLANO PESTO-GLAZED HALIBUT

Snapper, bass, thick sole or orange roughy can be substituted.

1	Poblano chile	1
3 Tbsp.	toasted, salted pepitas (pumpkin seeds)	45 mL
2	garlic cloves	2
1/4 c.	firmly packed fresh cilantro leaves	60 mL
1/2 c.	firmly packed Italian parsley leaves	125 mL
1 Tbsp.	fresh lime juice	15 mL
1 Tbsp.	olive oil	15 mL
	Salt and freshly ground black pepper	
2 Tbsp.	mayonnaise	30 mL
4	fresh halibut fillets or steaks	4
	(6 oz/375 g each)	
	Cilantro leaves for garnish	

Place chile on a broiler pan or a barbecue grill; broil approximately 3" (7.5 cm) from heat until skin is blistered and slightly charred on all sides, using tongs to turn. Place chile in a brown paper bag; close it tightly. Let rest for 10 minutes. Remove from bag. Peel off charred skin with your fingers. Make a slit in the chile; core; cut off stem; scrape out seeds and ribs. Cut chile in half; reserve one half for another purpose. Chop the other half.

With the motor running, add the roasted chile half, pepitas, and garlic to a blender or food processor fitted with metal blade. Process until puréed. Add cilantro, parsley and lime juice; process until finely chopped. With the motor running, slowly add olive oil in a fine stream. Add salt and pepper; taste for seasoning. Spoon pesto into a small bowl; add mayonnaise; stir well to combine.

Preheat broiler. Lightly spray a shallow broiler pan. Arrange fish, upside down, on pan and season with salt and pepper. Broil about 3"(7.5 cm) from heat for 3 minutes. Carefully turn fish, using a spatula; spread desired amount of mayonnaise pesto mixture evenly over fish. Return to broiler and broil about 3 more minutes until bubbly, well-browned, and fish flakes easily with a fork.

MAKES: 4 servings and about 1/2 c. (125 mL) pesto (Reserve any remaining pesto in a well-sealed container in the refrigerator.)

Serving suggestion: Delicious with a basket of toasted tortilla chips and a mixture of roasted bell peppers.

Wine suggestion: Minerally white: '95 Domaine Laroche Chablis Les Vaudevey 1er Cru, France $$$

SAUTEED SCALLOPS WITH ZUCCHINI AND MUSHROOMS

Sea scallops are preferred for their sweet meatiness. Rock shrimp or prawns can be substituted for the scallops.

2 Tbsp.	unsalted butter, divided	30 mL
2 Tbsp.	olive oil, divided	30 mL
2	small zucchini, julienned	2
2	small summer squash, julienned	2
6	medium mushrooms, julienned	6
2	garlic cloves, minced	2
2 Tbsp.	finely chopped fresh basil	30 mL
	Salt and freshly ground black pepper	
1^{1}/$_2$ lb.	sea or bay scallops	750 g
1^{1}/$_2$ Tbsp.	fresh lemon juice	25 mL
1 tsp.	finely chopped lemon peel	5 mL
1 Tbsp.	chopped fresh parsley	15 mL

Heat 1 Tbsp. (15 mL) butter and 1 Tbsp. (15 mL) olive oil in a large skillet on medium-high. Add zucchini, squash and mushrooms; sauté about 3 minutes or until they are just tender, stirring occasionally to evenly distribute. Add garlic, basil, salt and pepper. Cook another minute; cover; remove from heat and reserve.

Meanwhile, cut sea scallops in half horizontally.

If using bay scallops, leave whole. Heat remaining butter and oil in another large skillet. Season scallops with salt and pepper. Add to pan in several batches and sauté over medium-high about 2 minutes on each side or until just tender. (Remove cooked scallops to a covered dish and continue cooking remaining scallops.) Return all scallops to pan, add lemon juice and peel; heat briefly, tossing scallops to coat them.

MAKES: 4 servings

Serving suggestion: To serve, spoon vegetables onto a heated platter. Spoon scallops on top. Sprinkle with parsley. Serve immediately with your favourite rice or pasta..

Wine suggestion: Big, toasty white: '96 Signorello Napa Valley Semillon, California $$$

Canada Post's 1963 15-cent stamp - four Canada geese in a blue and white design - was painted on canoe canvas by Ducks Unlimited Canada artist Angus Shortt.

FRESH SALMON CREPES WITH TARRAGON SAUCE

Poached sea bass or trout can be substituted for the salmon.

1 lb.	boneless salmon fillet	500 g
	Water	
	Grated peel and juice of 1 lemon	
6 Tbsp.	butter or margarine	90 mL
1	shallot, minced	1
10	button mushrooms, sliced	10
6 Tbsp.	flour	90 mL
2 c.	1% milk	500 mL
2 Tbsp.	Dijon mustard	30 mL
1/4 tsp.	salt	2 mL
1/2 tsp.	white pepper	3 mL
2 c.	fish cooking liquid	500 mL
2 Tbsp.	minced fresh tarragon	30 mL
2/3 c.	grated Gruyère cheese, divided	150 mL
8	crêpes	8

Place fish in a large skillet, covered with water. Add grated peel and juice. Cover; bring to a slow boil; reduce heat to simmer for 3-4 minutes or until cooked through. Remove fish and measure liquid (you'll need 2 c./500 mL). Discard remaining liquid. In a medium saucepan, heat butter until bubbly. Add shallot and mushrooms; sauté until shallot is soft and mushrooms are starting to colour. With a slotted spoon, remove shallot and mushrooms to a medium bowl. Stir flour into butter in pan. Stir and cook 1 minute. Stir in milk; stir and cook until you have a smooth thickened sauce. Stir in mustard, salt, pepper, cooking liquid, tarragon and half the cheese. When sauce is smooth and hot, remove from heat.

Measure 1 1/2 c. (375 mL) sauce into the bowl with the mushrooms. Flake fish into chunks; add to bowl. Mix gently to combine. Place 8 crêpes, browned side down, on counter. Divide filling among crêpes; roll each over filling, placing with seam side down in individual bakers or on oven-proof dinner plates, two per person.

Add remaining cheese to remaining sauce. Pour over top of all crêpes. Place under a preheated broiler about 5" (12.5 cm) away from heat; broil until browned on top and very hot.

MAKES: 4 servings

Serving suggestion: Delicious with a crisp salad and hot crusty bread or rolls.

Wine suggestion: Zesty sparkling: Gloria Ferrer Sonoma Brut, California $$

GRILLED SWORDFISH
ON A BED OF SPICY CABBAGE

Tuna or shark can be substituted for the swordfish.

1 Tbsp.	fresh lime juice	15 mL
2 Tbsp.	rice vinegar	30 mL
1 Tbsp.	finely chopped fresh ginger	15 mL
1 Tbsp.	finely chopped green onions	15 mL
3 Tbsp.	vegetable oil	45 mL
1 Tbsp.	soy sauce	15 mL
	Freshly ground black pepper	
4	(1/3-1/2 lb./165-250 g) swordfish steaks, 4 no more than 3/4" (1.80 cm) thick	
3 Tbsp.	vegetable oil	45 mL
1	leek, finely chopped	1
2	carrots, peeled, julienned	2
1/2	red bell pepper, seeded , julienned	1/2
1	medium green cabbage, cored, finely shredded*	1
1 tsp.	chili paste with garlic	5 mL
2 Tbsp.	soy sauce	30 mL
1/4 c.	dry sherry	60 mL
	Salt and pepper to taste	
2 Tbsp.	toasted pine nuts	30 mL

Savoy cabbage is best.

Combine first 7 ingredients. Whisk until blended. Arrange fish in shallow glass dish; pour marinade over. Turn pieces to coat. Marinate fish up to 4 hours in the refrigerator, covered.

In a skillet, heat oil on medium-high until hot. Cook leek for about 1-2 minutes or until slightly softened. Add carrots and red bell pepper; cook for 2 more minutes, stirring occasionally. Add cabbage; cook 3 minutes longer or until just wilted. Add chili paste, soy sauce, sherry and salt and pepper to taste. Stir to combine and bring to a boil; cook for another minute. Taste for seasoning; add pine nuts. Set aside and keep warm while grilling fish.

Prepare barbecue or broiler for medium-heat cooking. Remove fish from marinade; grill about 3" (7.5 cm) from heat 3-5 minutes on each side, depending on the thickness or until desired doneness.

MAKES: 4 servings

Serving suggestion: Spoon cabbage mixture onto each serving plate; place swordfish on top of cabbage.

Wine suggestion: Spicy red: '94 Marqués de Riscal Tinto Reserva, Spain $$

MUSSELS MARINIÈRE

Clams or swimming scallops in their shells can be substituted for the mussels.

2 c.	dry white wine	500 mL
6	shallots, minced	6
1	bay leaf	1
1/4 c.	finely chopped fresh parsley, divided	60 mL
	Freshly ground black pepper	
6 Tbsp.	unsalted butter	90 mL
4 lb.	mussels, well cleaned and scrubbed	2 kg

Bring wine, shallots, bay leaf, 2 Tbsp. (30 mL) parsley, black pepper and butter to a boil in a very large stock pot on high heat for about 4-5 minutes. Add cleaned mussels; cover tightly; steam them until they open, about 5 minutes. Hold stock pot with both handles and shake the mussels so that they can cook evenly. Discard any mussels which do not open. Spoon mussels into large soup bowls, spoon broth over them and sprinkle with the remaining parsley. Serve immediately. (You can also add 1 c. (250 mL) of fresh bread crumbs to the stock mixture when boiling to give broth a thicker texture, if desired.)

MAKES: 6 appetizer servings or 2-4 entrée servings

Serving suggestion: These classically prepared mussels are delicious served with crusty French bread and a large crisp salad.

Wine suggestion: Bone-dry, citrusy white: Ca'Bolani Frizzante Pinot Chardonnay, Italy $

SALMON RISOTTO WITH ASPARAGUS

1 lb.	boneless salmon fillet	500 g
2 c.	chicken/fish/vegetable broth	500 mL
5 Tbsp.	unsalted butter, divided	75 mL
1	medium onion, diced	1
3	large garlic cloves, minced	3
	Chicken/fish/vegetable broth	
3/4 lb.	fresh asparagus, diagonally cut	375 g
1 1/4 c.	arborio (short grain) rice	310 mL
1 c.	white wine	250 mL
1/4 tsp.	salt	2 mL
1/2 tsp.	white pepper	3 mL
	Grated peel and juice of 1 lemon	
1-2 Tbsp.	minced fresh dill	15-30 mL

Place fish in a shallow baker (for the microwave) or a skillet (for the stove). Cover with 2 c. (500 mL) chicken/fish/vegetable broth. Poach 4-5 minutes or until cooked through. Drain fish, flake; measure liquid. (This can be done ahead of time.) Meanwhile, heat 3 Tbsp. (45 mL) butter in a large saucepan until hot. Add onion and garlic, sauté until onion softens. Add additional broth to fish cooking liquid to make it up to 3 c. (750 mL). Heat to a strong simmer; add asparagus pieces. Cook 2-3 minutes.

Remove with slotted spoon. Keep broth hot. Meanwhile, add rice to saucepan. Stir until rice is coated with butter. Add wine slowly, stirring constantly. When wine has been absorbed, add hot fish cooking liquid/broth mixture slowly, one ladle at a time, stirring constantly. Only add more after each amount has been absorbed. The rice mixture will start to get very soft and creamy. Stir in salt, pepper, lemon peel and juice, dill and asparagus. When all liquid has been absorbed, gently stir in salmon chunks. Heat 1 minute; stir in remaining 2 Tbsp. (30mL) butter; serve at once.

MAKES: 4 servings

Serving suggestion: Delicious with a sliced tomato/red onion salad.

Wine suggestion: Zesty white: '96 Fazzi Bataglia Verdicchio dei Castelli di Jesi Classico, Italy $

HALIBUT CHEEKS WITH HOMEMADE KETCHUP

Any batter or any firm white fish can be substituted. The ketchup will keep, covered, in the fridge for up to 1 month. Works well with fried oysters too.

Ketchup

4 lbs.	Roma tomatoes, cored, seeded, quartered	4
2 c.	diced onions	500 mL
6	garlic cloves, minced	6
1 1/2 c.	packed brown sugar	375 mL
1 1/2 c.	tarragon vinegar	375 mL
6 Tbsp.	pickling spice	90 mL
1	Jalapeño pepper, seeded, minced	1
1 tsp.	dried red chiles	5 mL
1 tsp.	salt	5 mL
1/2 tsp.	dry mustard	3 mL

Batter

2 c.	buttermilk pancake mix*	500 mL
1/4 tsp.	ground pepper	2 mL
	Grated peel of 1 lemon	
1 Tbsp.	minced fresh herbs (optional)	15 mL
1-1 1/4 c.	flat beer or ale	250-310 mL
2 lbs.	halibut cheeks	1 kg

* Use a mix that only requires water.

Combine all ketchup ingredients in a large Dutch oven. Cook over medium heat about 2 1/2 hours or until quite thick. Purée in a food processor; then push through a fine sieve.

To make the batter, combine the pancake mix, pepper, peel and herbs (if using) in a large bowl; mix well. Mix in beer. If you are using within half an hour, you will likely only need the 1 c. (250 mL) to make the batter the desired consistency. If you want to put the batter in the refrigerator overnight or for several hours, you will probably need the 1 1/4 c. (310 mL). Make to desired consistency.

Heat at least 3" (7.5 cm) oil in a deep fat fryer or in a deep saucepan until 365°F. (185°C). Dip halibut cheeks in batter to completely coat. Drop carefully into hot oil. Cook, turning halfway, about 2-3 minutes or until a deep golden brown. Drain on paper towel. Serve at once with homemade ketchup.

MAKES: 4 servings

Serving suggestion: Traditional with french fries and peas.

Wine suggestion: Grapey red: '96 Hardy Bankside Shiraz, Australia $

THAI CRABCAKES WITH CHILE CILANTRO SAUCE

Chile Cilantro Sauce

1/3 c.	peanut butter	75 mL
2 Tbsp.	soy sauce	30 mL
1/2 tsp.	dried red chiles	3 mL
2 Tbsp.	lime juice	30 mL
1/2 c.	plain yoghurt	125 mL
1/3 c.	chopped fresh cilantro	75 mL

Crabcakes

3 Tbsp.	vegetable oil, divided	45 mL
1/4 c.	chopped green onion	60 mL
3	garlic cloves, minced	3
1 Tbsp.	chopped fresh ginger	15 mL
1	green chile, seeded and minced	1
1 tsp.	grated lemon peel	5 mL
1¼ lb.	cooked crabmeat	625 g
2/3 c.	mayonnaise	150 mL
1/2 c.	fresh bread crumbs	125 mL
1/3 c.	chopped fresh cilantro	75 mL
1/4 c.	chopped fresh mint	60 mL
1 tsp.	sesame oil	5 mL
1/4 tsp.	*each* salt and pepper	2 mL

In bowl, whisk together all sauce ingredients; set aside.

MAKES: about 1 c. (250 mL)

In large skillet, heat 1 Tbsp. (15 mL) oil over medium-high heat. Cook green onions, garlic, ginger, chile and lemon peel for 3 minutes.

Squeeze crabmeat very dry. In large bowl, combine crab, mayonnaise, bread crumbs, cilantro, mint, sesame oil, salt and pepper and green onion mixture. Shape into 16 small or 8 large balls.

Heat remaining oil in non-stick skillet over medium-high heat. Sauté crabcakes, pressing with back of spatula to flatten each to about 1/2" (1.25 cm) thick, in batches, for 3 minutes per side or until golden brown and cooked through. Add more oil if necessary during the cooking. Drain on paper towels. Serve with Chile Cilantro Sauce.

MAKES: 16 small or 8 large crabcakes

Serving suggestion: Add a cold rice/sugar pea salad.

Wine suggestion: Honeyed, spicy white: '97 Hugel Gentil, Alsace, France $$

SOLE PICATTA WITH LEMON, PARSLEY AND CAPERS

The sole can be substituted with orange roughy, trout, snapper, cod, catfish or bass. The cooking times will vary with the thickness of the fish. This very quick dish is full of flavour. You can replace the butter with olive oil if you're watching your cholesterol.

1/4 c.	flour	60 mL
	Salt and pepper	
1 lb.	sole fillets, cleaned and wiped	500 g
2 Tbsp.	unsalted butter	30 mL
1 Tbsp.	olive oil	15 mL
3 Tbsp.	lemon juice	45 mL
1½ Tbsp.	drained and rinsed capers	25 mL
2 Tbsp.	finely chopped parsley	30 mL

In a plastic bag combine the flour, salt and pepper. Place fillets in bag and shake until evenly coated.

In a large skillet heat butter and oil on medium-high. Arrange fillets in skillet; sauté about 2 minutes on the first side and 1 minute on the second or until just tender when pierced with a fork. (You need to do this in batches.) Set cooked fillets aside, covered. When all fillets are cooked and removed to a side plate, add lemon juice, capers and parsley to the skillet; mix to combine for a minute. Place fillets on hot serving plates and spoon over the lemon caper sauce. Serve immediately.

MAKES: 2 servings

Serving suggestion: Goes well with a herbed vegetable rice or baby roast potatoes.

Wine suggestion: Smooth, citrusy white: '96 Jaffelin Bourgogne Aligoté, Burgundy, France $

FINISHING TOUCHES

FINISHING TOUCHES

MARSH MARIGOLDS AND PRAIRIE CLOVER

Ecosystem: a complex ecological community, such as grassland, desert or rain forest, where organisms and environment sustain each other.

The ecosystems of North America's prairies began to evolve 16,000 years ago, in the wake of the glaciers. These mammoth sheets of ice left behind them landscapes studded with wetlands – lakes, marshes, rivers. To a botanist, wetlands are filled with riches of the floral species – cattails and pussy willows, bulrushes and pitcher plants and forget-me-nots, water lilies and marsh marigolds, wild rice and St. John's wort. There are more than 250 species of grass, flowers and shrubs in Ducks Unlimited country, species that have continued to bloom through flood and drought, prairie fire and blizzard. These are tough plants.

Wetlands are essential to all life forms, as they purify toxins, filter ground and surface water, and act as giant sponges to help control floods. They are natural treatment facilities, breaking down nitrates and phosphates, cleansing water of sewage, pesticides, heavy metals and fertilizers. Dirty water in, clean water out.

YOUR OWN BOG GARDEN

Tramping through a marshy area in the south of England on a recent summer, following the path poet-priest George Herbert walked from his vicarage to Salisbury Cathedral, hikers were charmed by the rising scent of wild mint, one of the edible and medicinal plants that thrive in the wetlands.

If you have a pond or bog or stream on your property, you may be able to grow a variety of edible plants, beginning with the mint to sauce your lamb. Among the more unusual are the creeping dogwood, which bears an edible fruit, and the water chestnut. Labrador tea, known to the Cree as muskeko-pukwa and the Chipewyan as wish-a-ca-pucca, is an ancient and still popular tonic. More familiar are watercress (a member of the mustard family), the berry siblings, blue and cran, and all of the mints – spear, pepper, apple and (yes) eau-de-cologne.

Wetlands occupy only 3.4 percent of the world's surface, but 24 percent of those wetlands are in Canada, forming 14 percent of the country's area. Unfortunately, Canadian wetlands have been depleted drastically. Over the last century and a half, Canada has lost 70 percent of its wetlands. In the United States, half of the country's original wetlands are gone. Ducks Unlimited has worked hard to create, restore and preserve wetlands, but it's an uphill battle. For every wetland Ducks Unlimited creates, two others might be drained for expanding urbanization and industrial or agricultural use.

Ducks Unlimited works also to reseed uplands – grassy areas adjoining wetlands, providing nesting cover for birds. Prairie CARE (Conservation of Agriculture, Resources and the Environment) is a program delivered by Ducks Unlimited and various Canadian and US governments to help landowners adopt soil and water conservation measures which benefit their objectives and improve wildlife habitat. Sometimes landowners call Ducks Unlimited to join the CARE program. "We see ourselves as a clearing house for habitat enhancement," says Ducks Unlimited biologist Duane Hudd. "We can get a project rolling in hours, even minutes."

As part of its program, Ducks Unlimited harvests native seeds and sows them in micro-environments from eroded knolls to wet meadows. Some of the plants are needlegrass, white and purple clover, porcupine grass, bluestem, western snowberry, reedgrass and basin wildrye. As long ago as 1939, William Leitch, then manager of Saskatchewan's Waterhen Marsh, planted bulrush and sago pondweed, brome grass and sweet clover. That year, there were two pairs of breeding geese at the marsh. By 1971, Bill Leitch's plants provided cover for 145 nests.

OUTWARD FROM OAK HAMMOCK AND WATERFOWL WAY

Central headquarters for Ducks Unlimited in Canada is the Oak Hammock Marsh Conservation Centre, outside Winnipeg, Manitoba, in the land of the Saulteaux people. Scots in Lord Selkirk's Red River settlement came here on outings in the 1880s. It was a popular picnic place, with giant oak trees – the only oaks for miles. People would bring hammocks and tie them between the trees. And so, the area became known as Oak Hammock Marsh.

A century later, after a massive restoration program initiated in 1967 by DU and federal and provincial governments, Oak Hammock is 14 square miles (36 square kilometres) of marshes, meadows, tall grass prairie, lure crops and aspen-oak bluffs. Managed by Manitoba Natural Resources, Oak Hammock is home to 280 species of birds and hundreds of species of mammals, reptiles, amphibians and insects, attracting 200,000 visitors annually. A visit to Oak Hammock Marsh is a fascinating experience for all ages. Through the year, there are a number of special tours, from stargazing and birding to exploring the marsh by van, voyageur canoe and snowshoe. There are also camps for youngsters – Marsh's Camp, for ages 7 to 11; Greenwing Camp for ages 12 to 14.

In the United States, Ducks Unlimited's principal offices can be found at One Waterfowl Way, Memphis, Tennessee. Here Ducks Unlimited is set in the centre of the Mississippi Flyway, surrounded by woods and wetlands, with nesting geese, cooing doves and grazing deer.

But Ducks Unlimited's activities reach far beyond Oak Hammock and Waterfowl Way. Ducks Unlimited has become a global leader in wildlife habitat conservation, sharing its expertise all over the world, from Africa to the Caribbean, South America to eastern Europe.

Ducks Unlimited began its work using horses, hand shovels, ploughs, mules and steam engines. Today, it uses satellite reconnaissance, radio technology, computer models and other advanced technology. But its focus and objectives remain the same: habitat conservation on a landscape basis. And untold numbers of living creatures are grateful—from the mangrove cuckoo to the nine-banded armadillo, from the leopard frog to the muskox, from the great blue heron to...us.

JOINING THE FLOCK

If reading this has made you feel you would like to join Ducks Unlimited, please know that individuals, children, corporations and foundations can all become partners with DU in its conservation projects. The fastest way to learn more: call 1-800-665-DUCK.

BLUEGRASS AND SUGAR CANE

"The Sea of Grass" was Conrad Richter's name for it – "that vast grazing empire which once covered the western part of North America from the great plains to the Rocky Mountains and beyond." You may still find Richter's novel in a bookshop or library, and Elia Kazan's film, full of wonderful images of waving grasslands, is available on videotape.

The word grass derives from the Middle English 'gras', which evolved from the Old English 'groes,' a word linked to the Old High German 'gras' and the Old English 'growan,' which means, simply and appropriately, 'to grow.'

The emergence of grasslands 25 million years ago changed the face of the earth, the animals that live on it, and the way we live. Without grass, which includes everything from corn to sugar cane, we would have no agriculture – no snap, crackle and pop in our cereal bowls, no rum in our punch, and, because there would be no grazing animals, no cream in our coffee.

Grasses rise to various heights, from just over one inch (three centimetres) to more than six and one-half feet (two metres). Crop grasses complete their life cycle in one year, but there are some grass species that thrive for centuries.

The great range wars were fought over grass – ranchers wanting the sea of grass left untouched, for their great herds of cattle to graze; farmers wanting to plough the land to plant wheat and barley, rye and oats. This has been the plot of innumerable works of fiction, from "Shane" to "Oklahoma!" (which told us "The Farmer and the Cowman Should Be Friends").

Grass has even given a name to a musical style: bluegrass, the pickin' and strummin' country music that originated in the bluegrass state of Kentucky and it has conservationists, too.

ROASTED RED PEPPER SMOKED OYSTER SOUP

This recipe has been adapted from the Smoked Oyster Soup served at the Oyster Creek Inn on Chuckanut Drive, Washington. Wonderful!

1/2 lb.	red bell pepper (about 1 large)	250 g.
	Olive oil	
1	(3 oz./85 g) tin smoked oysters	1
3 Tbsp.	tomato paste	45 mL
4 c.	fish broth *	1 L
1¹/₂ Tbsp.	lemon juice	25 mL
2 Tbsp.	dry white wine	30 mL
1/4 -1/2 tsp.	Tabasco	1-2 mL
1/8 tsp.	cayenne	0.5 mL
1/4 -1/2 tsp.	salt	1-2 mL
1/4 tsp.	ground white pepper	1 mL
3 Tbsp.	soft butter	45 mL
3 Tbsp.	flour	45 mL

**Prepare from cubes; buy fresh or frozen. If unavailable, use clam nectar or chicken broth.*

Preheat broiler. Cut pepper in half; discard core and seeds. Place, skin side up, on a baking sheet; brush lightly with olive oil; broil until blackened. Immediately place pepper in a paper bag; close bag and let stand until cold. Pull off blackened skin and place pepper pieces in food processor.

Add oysters (undrained) and tomato paste to processor; process until smooth. (Press through a fine sieve if you want it very smooth.) Combine purée and fish broth in a large saucepan over medium heat. When hot, stir in lemon juice, wine, Tabasco, cayenne, salt and pepper.

Mix together soft butter and flour to make a beurre manié or paste. Stirring constantly (preferably with a wire whisk), beat in paste, a spoonful at a time. Continue cooking over medium high until soup thickens slightly and is bubbly (about 3-5 minutes).

MAKES: 4-6 servings

Serving suggestion: Serve at once with a swirl of yoghurt and chopped chives on top, if desired.

Wine suggestion: Zesty, honeyed bubbly: Deinhard Lila Imperial Riesling (Sekt), Germany $

ROASTED CHÈVRE STACKS WITH MANGO/PAPAYA COULIS

This recipe is our version of a splendid appetizer at "House Piccolo" on Saltspring Island, British Columbia.

1	small ripe papaya, seeded*	1
1	small ripe mango, seeded	1
	Salt, to taste	
1 Tbsp.	sugar	15 mL
2	(4oz./113 g) pkg. French Chèvre (Goat Cheese)**	2
	Coarse ground black pepper	
4	slices lean bacon	4
1	(10 oz./283g) pkg. fresh spinach, stems removed, washed, dried	1
1 Tbsp.	Balsamic vinegar	15 mL
	Salt and pepper, to taste	

** Strawberry papaya is best if you can find one.*
*** French Chèvre has the best flavour and texture for this dish.*

Peel papaya and mango; process in a food processor until very smooth; stir in salt and sugar. Set fruit coulis aside. Slice the two logs of Chèvre into 4 slices to give 8 slices total. Roll the edges of each in the black pepper. Place on baking sheet. Preheat oven to 350ºF. (180ºC).

Cook bacon in a large skillet until crisp; remove and chop. Set aside. Tear cleaned spinach leaves into small pieces. Add to hot bacon fat in skillet; cook over medium heat for about 1 minute, tossing with tongs until wilted and about half-cooked. Stir in Balsamic vinegar, salt and pepper and bacon. Remove from heat.

Place baking sheet of Chèvre in oven for about 3-4 minutes or until hot but not melting. Pour fruit coulis onto four plates; tilt plates to spread evenly into a pool. Use tongs to place small mounds of cooked spinach mixture in the centre of each plate. Place two slices of baked chèvre on top of each spinach mound, tilting one against the other. Serve at once.

MAKES: 4 servings

Serving suggestion: Add fresh berries to the plate for decoration.

Wine suggestion: Citrusy white: '95 Oyster Bay Sauvignon Blanc, New Zealand $

FINISHING TOUCHES

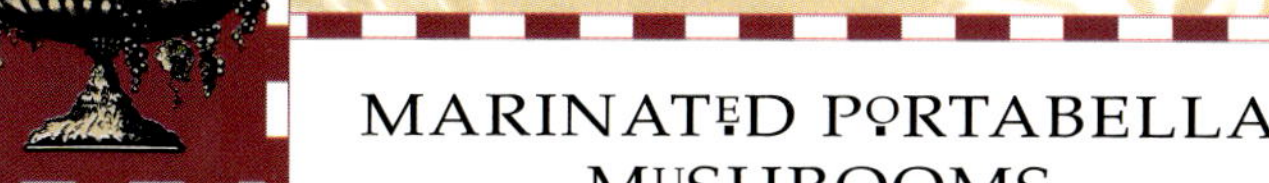

PENNE IN SUN-DRIED TOMATO CREAM

Any pasta can be substituted.

3/4 lb.	dried penne pasta	375 g
2 Tbsp.	oil from sun-dried tomatoes	30 mL
1	medium onion, minced	1
1	carrot, peeled, minced	1
1	celery stalk with leaves, diced	1
4	garlic cloves, minced	4
1/2 c.	sun-dried tomatoes, drained, chopped	125 mL
1	(28 fl. oz./796 mL) tin chopped plum tomatoes	1
2 Tbsp.	tomato paste	30 mL
1/2 c.	chopped fresh parsley	125 mL
1 Tbsp.	minced fresh basil	15 mL
1 Tbsp.	minced fresh thyme	15 mL
1 c.	light cream	250 mL
1	(10 fl. oz./284 mL) tin chicken broth	1
1 Tbsp.	flour	15 mL
	Freshly grated Asiago or Parmesan cheese	

Cook penne in a large pot of boiling salted water until tender but not soft. Drain, rinse, reserve.

Heat oil in a large skillet until hot. Add onion, carrot, celery, garlic and sun-dried tomatoes. Cook, stirring occasionally until onion is softened. Add tomatoes and tomato paste. Stir to combine; cook 10 minutes, uncovered, to reduce liquid. Add parsley, basil and thyme. You can purée the sauce in a food processor at this point if you wish. Then return to the skillet. Mix together cream, broth and flour; stir into skillet contents. Cook and stir another minute until hot and thickened. Do not boil. Add pasta; toss to coat.

MAKES: 4 servings

Serving suggestion: Serve at once on hot plates with grated Asiago or Parmesan cheese over top and a crisp salad alongside.

Wine suggestion: Round, spicy red: '96 Moculta Shiraz Barossa Valley, Australia $$

> *Saskatchewan, with its particular combination of water and grasslands, is critically important in any meaningful waterfowl conservation program on the North American continent. Since DUC began operations in the province in 1938, it has invested over $75 million to construct and maintain more than 4,000 marshland projects, all of which serve to improve the conditions for ducks to breed, nest and raise their broods or migrate.*

MARINATED PORTABELLA MUSHROOMS

1 1/2 Tbsp.	minced fresh garlic	25 mL
1	shallot, minced	1
2 tsp.	Dijon mustard	10 mL
2/3 c.	red wine vinegar	150 mL
1/3 c.	mixed minced fresh herbs (rosemary, thyme, basil, tarragon)	75 mL
1 1/3 c.	extra virgin olive oil	325 mL
8	large Portabella mushrooms	8
	Asiago cheese (*optional*)	

Mix together the first 6 ingredients in a large deep bowl, whisking until well combined. Add mushrooms that have been wiped and which have had their stems removed. If mushrooms are too large to easily sit in the marinade, cut in half. Cover bowl; marinate on the counter at least 4 hours, turning several times to fully coat each piece with marinade.

Preheat broiler or barbecue. Broil or barbecue mushroom pieces about 4 minutes each side or until bubbly and browned. Brush with marinade as you turn them over. Discard unused marinade.

MAKES: 4 servings

Serving suggestion: Serve with wedges or circles of sautéed polenta with large shards of Asiago cheese tossed on top.

Wine suggestion: Buttery white: '95 Rosemount Estate Show Reserve Chardonnay, Australia $$

GNOCCHI WITH CREAMY PESTO SAUCE

2 lbs.	baking potatoes, cooked	1 kg
1	egg	1
1 3/4 c.	flour	425 mL
1/4 c.	grated Parmesan cheese	60 mL
	Salt and white pepper, to taste	
	Instant flour (optional)	

Sauce

1 c.	packed fresh basil leaves	250 mL
3 Tbsp.	pine nuts	45 mL
	Salt and pepper, to taste	
3	peeled garlic cloves	3
1/4 c.	grated Parmesan cheese	60 mL
1/4 c.	extra virgin olive oil	60 mL
1/2 c.	whipping cream	125 mL
	Asiago or Parmesan cheese	

Combine gnocci ingredients except instant flour. Mix or beat together until well-blended. Refrigerate 15 minutes. (Longer if the potatoes were still warm when you mixed them.)

Combine all sauce ingredients except whipping cream and Asiago/Parmesan cheese in a food processor.

Process until smooth. Refrigerate pesto until needed.

Roll handsful of the gnocchi mixture into long rolls (using the instant flour on the board) about 3/4"(2 cm) thick. With a sharp unserrated knife, cut into logs about 3/4"(2 cm) long. Using both hands, implant one finger in one side of each piece to make a small dimple while rolling the other side across the tines of a fork to make stripes or ridges. Keep coated with instant flour on board as you bring a large pot of water to a boil. Drop gnocchi, a few at a time, into the boiling water. After about 2 minutes they should float to the top. Remove with a slotted spoon to a plate in a single layer. Continue until all are cooked.

Meanwhile, heat whipping cream in a large skillet to a boil. Add the pesto; stir until well-blended. Boil and stir about 4 minutes or until sauce thickens and coats a spoon thickly. Add gnocchi to skillet (or combine with sauce in a large bowl). Stir to mix; serve at once.

MAKES: 4 servings

Serving suggestion: Serve at once on hot plates with large shards of Asiago or Parmesan cheese over top and extra basil leaves.

Wine suggestion: Crisp, citrusy white: '97 Banrock Station Unwooded Chardonnay, Australia $

BULGAR WHEAT SALAD WITH TOMATOES AND OLIVES

1 c.	bulgar wheat	250 mL
1/2 c.	chopped fresh parsley	125 mL
3	green onions, chopped	3
1 c.	frozen peas	250 mL
2	ripe tomatoes, seeded, chopped	2
3 Tbsp.	chopped fresh mint	45 mL
1	(4.5 fl. oz./125 mL) tin sliced black olives, drained	1
2	ripe avocados, peeled, diced	2
	Grated peel and juice of 1 large lime	
2 Tbsp.	red wine vinegar	30 mL
3/4 tsp.	salt	4 mL
3/4 tsp.	coarse black pepper	4 mL
1 tsp.	minced fresh garlic	5 mL
1/4 c.	extra virgin olive oil	60 mL
	Fresh orange segments OR papaya slices *(optional)*	

Cover wheat with boiling water in a medium bowl. Let stand 1/2 hour. Drain; squeeze dry; place in a large bowl. Add next 7 ingredients. Mix gently. Whisk together following 6 dressing ingredients; pour over salad. Mix gently to fully coat all ingredients.

Refrigerate until serving. Mix well before portioning

MAKES: 4 servings

Serving suggestion: Serve on cold plates with orange segments or papaya slices.

Wine suggestion: Plummy red: '96 Concha y Toro Trio Merlot, Chile $

CRAB AND SHRIMP CAKES WITH ROASTED PEPPER AIOLI

Cakes

3/4 lb.	fresh crabmeat	375 g
1/2 lb.	fresh cooked shrimp, roughly chopped	250 g
1/2 c.	fine dry bread crumbs	125 mL
1	egg, beaten	1
1/4 c.	*each* finely minced red onion, red and yellow bell pepper	60 mL
1	Jalapeño pepper, seeded, minced	1
2 Tbsp.	chopped fresh oregano	30 mL
1/2 tsp.	black pepper	3 mL
	Salt, to taste	
1/3 c.	sour cream	75 mL

Aioli

1	large red bell pepper, halved, seeded	1
1	large Jalapeño pepper, halved, seeded	1
1 c.	*each* mayonnaise and sour cream	250 mL
1 Tbsp.	Balsamic vinegar	15 mL
1 Tbsp.	*each* minced fresh oregano and fresh garlic	15 mL
1/2 c.	fine dry bread crumbs	125 mL

Combine all crab cake ingredients in a large bowl; mix very well to combine. Using your hands, shape into 12 patties (small and thick rather than larger and thin), pressing mixture together very firmly. Place on a plate; cover with plastic wrap; refrigerate at least 2 hours or up to overnight until ready to cook.

To make the aioli: place the red bell pepper halves and the Jalapeño halves, cut side down, on a baking sheet under a broiler. Broil until very black. Place in a small paper bag until cool. Rub off blackened skins; place peppers in a food processor with the 5 remaining aioli ingredients. Process until smooth. Cover and refrigerate until 1/2 hour before serving. (Any extra can be refrigerated 1 week.)

When ready to cook the cakes, heat butter or margarine in a large skillet until bubbly (do not place cakes in the skillet until the butter is hot). Pour the 1/2 c. (125 mL) fine dry crumbs onto a piece of waxed paper; coat each crab cake with the crumbs, pressing on firmly on all sides. Place in the hot butter or margarine, a few at a time. Sauté on both sides, turning carefully, until golden brown and sizzling. Serve at once with the room temperature aioli sauce.

MAKES: 4 entrée servings or 6-12 appetizer servings

Serving suggestion: Delicious served with cold mixed mesclun salad greens as an appetizer or with vegetables as an entrée.

Wine suggestion: Honeyed white: '96 Rudolf Müller Piesporter Goldtröfchen Riesling Kabinett, Germany $$

THREE COCKTAILS

Sidecar

1	part brandy	1
1	part fresh lemon juice	1
1	part orange liqueur	1
	Ice cubes	
	Sugar	

Combine first three ingredients in a blender or cocktail shaker. Process until blended. Add one ice cube per drink. Process again. Dip rims of glasses into water or lemon juice and then into sugar to make a sugar-coated rim. Fill glasses with ice cubes and pour drink over top. Serve at once.

Daiquiri

1	part amber rum	1
1	part fresh lime juice	1
1/2	part sugar syrup *	1/2
	Ice cubes	
	Lime slices	

** Make sugar syrup to keep in the fridge for future drinks. (or hummingbird food!) Mix together 1 part sugar and 1 part very hot water. Stir until dissolved. Keep refrigerated.*

Combine rum, juice and syrup in a blender or cocktail shaker. Add one ice cube per drink. Process again. Fill glasses with ice cubes and pour drink over top. Serve with lime slice on rim of each glass.

Pimm's Cup

1	jigger Pimm's #1	1
	Ice cubes	
	Lemonade, ginger ale or 7-Up	
	Cucumber slices or spears	
	Orange slices	
	Mint sprigs	

Pour Pimm's into each glass. Add ice cubes and fill with lemonade, ginger ale, or 7-Up. Stir. Top each glass with a spear of cucumber, orange slice and mint sprig.

Migrating birds such as geese honk to keep the skein in line. And birds communicate not only by calls, but by body language, including tail and wing flicking, ruffling of feathers, crouching and movements of eyes and beaks. Many normal comfort movements like stretching and preening have been ritualized into means of communication for courtship, territorial offense and social dominance.

BRANDIED CARROT SOUP

3 Tbsp.	olive oil	45 mL
2	medium onions, diced	2
4 c.	diced carrots (about 9 large)	1 L
6	garlic cloves, minced	6
2	celery stalks with leaves, chopped	2
4 c.	chicken broth	1 L
1 Tbsp.	tomato paste	15 mL
1/2 c.	instant potato flakes	125 mL
1 Tbsp.	grated orange peel	15 mL
1/2 tsp.	salt	3 mL
3/4 tsp.	white pepper	4 mL
1/4 c.	brandy	60 mL
1 c.	light cream	250 mL

Heat oil in a large Dutch oven until hot. Add onion, carrots, garlic and celery; cook, stirring occasionally, until carrots are starting to soften. Add broth, tomato paste, instant potato flakes and seasonings. Tilt lid, reduce heat to a simmer. Cook 15 minutes or until carrots are totally soft. Stir in brandy. Let cool until easy to handle in a food processor. Purée until smooth. (The soup can be left like this or you can push it through a fine sieve to make it even smoother.) Return to the heat. Stir in cream.

DO NOT BOIL after adding cream. Heat gently and serve at once in heated bowls. (Can be frozen before adding the cream.)

MAKES: 6 servings

Serving suggestion: Serve with the cold bulgar salad on page 77 for a delicious meatless supper.

Wine suggestion: Tangy dry madeira: Cossart & Gordon Sercial Dry Madeira 5 yr old, Portugal $

When the glaciers retreated thousands of years ago, they left the Manitoba landscape riddled with a multitude of productive wetlands. Perfect for waterfowl, these various types of wetlands support a wide variety of breeding birds, insects, mammals, reptiles and amphibians. In Manitoba alone, however, more than 70% of the original Prairie wetlands have been lost to economic development and land use changes Bird and animal populations have declined as a result. DU has secured more than 2,400 project segments across Manitoba.

PHYLLO PACKETS WITH GRUYERE AND TAPANADE

Tapanade

1	(6 oz./170 g) tin pitted black olives, drained	1
1/2 c.	pitted large green Sicilian olives	125 mL
1 Tbsp.	anchovy paste	15 mL
3 Tbsp.	drained capers	45 mL
	Grated peel and juice of 1/2 lemon	
5	sun-dried tomatoes, drained of oil	5
1 1/2 tsp.	minced fresh thyme	8 mL
2 Tbsp.	minced fresh basil	30 mL
	Salt and pepper, to taste	

Packets

1/2 lb.	Swiss Gruyère cheese	250 g
	Melted butter	
9	sheets phyllo pastry	9

Combine all tapanade ingredients in a food processor; process with pulse setting until combined but still coarse in texture. Set aside.

Cut cheese into 27 tiny cubes. Set aside. Melt some butter (about 1/3 c./75 mL). Assemble soft pastry brush, the tapanade and the phyllo pastry sheets. Keep those pastry sheets not being used in a towel while you work. (They dry out quickly.)

Preheat oven to 400ºF. (200ºC). Place first phyllo sheet on counter, vertical to you. With an unserrated knife, cut downwards into 3 columns. Brush each column lightly with melted butter. Place a cube of cheese at the bottom of each column. Top cheese with about 1/2-3/4 Tbsp. (8-10 mL) tapanade. Fold bottom left corner to right, over filling, making a triangle; continue back and forth up the column (as in spanakopittas) until you have a triangle package with several layers of pastry filled with cheese and tapanade. Place on a no-stick or sprayed baking sheet. When all cheese, pastry and tapanade have been used, brush each triangle with melted butter. Bake about 8-10 minutes or until golden brown and crisp. Serve at once.

MAKES: 6-8 servings

Serving suggestion: Serve on platters with other hors d'ouvres or on lettuce leaves on plates as an appetizer course.

Wine suggestion: Honeyed sparkling: Henkell Trocken Sparkling, Germany $

WILD MUSHROOM AND ROASTED GARLIC SOUP

3	heads garlic	3
2 Tbsp.	olive oil, divided	30 mL
	Chopped fresh oregano	
	Salt and pepper	
3/4 c.	barley	175 mL
1 1/2 c.	water	375 mL
3 Tbsp.	butter	45 mL
2	medium onions, chopped	2
2	large carrots, chopped	2
2 lbs.	Portabella mushrooms and button mushrooms, mixed, diced	1 kg
4	(10 fl. oz./284 mL) tins beef broth	4
2 Tbsp.	chopped fresh oregano	30 mL
2 Tbsp.	chopped fresh parsley	30 mL
1 Tbsp.	chopped fresh rosemary	15 mL

Preheat oven to 350ºF. (180ºC). Slice tops off garlic heads; place in a piece of foil. Drizzle with half the olive oil; sprinkle with chopped oregano and salt and pepper. Seal foil packet; bake about 3/4 hour. When cool, press garlic out of heads and mash. Boil barley in the water in a small saucepan for 1/2 hour. Reserve both water and barley.

Heat butter in a Dutch oven until hot. Add onion and carrot; sauté until tender. Heat remaining oil in large skillet until hot; add mushrooms and cook over high heat, stirring occasionally, until tender and the liquid has been reabsorbed. Remove from heat. Add broth to the Dutch oven. Simmer onion and carrot in broth until very soft (about 5 minutes). Purée the onion and carrot mixture in a food processor or use a hand-held blender. Return to Dutch oven. Purée half the mushrooms; add all mushrooms to Dutch oven. Replace over medium heat. Stir in mashed roasted garlic, barley and its cooking water. Simmer soup over low heat with lid tilted until barley is totally cooked (about 1/2 hour).

Stir in three chopped herbs; serve after about 1 minute.

MAKES: 8 servings

Serving suggestion: Perfect with hot cheese bread and our Green Goddess Salad.

Wine suggestion: Earthy red: '96 Adelsheim Pinot Noir, Oregon $$

NOTE: Any full-flavoured mushrooms can be used.

GREEN GODDESS SALAD

1 c.	commercial mayonnaise	250 mL
1/2 c.	sour cream	125 mL
1/3 c.	minced fresh parsley	75 mL
3 Tbsp.	minced green onion	45 mL
1	bunch watercress, roughly chopped	1
1 Tbsp.	minced fresh tarragon	15 mL
1 Tbsp.	fresh lemon juice	15 mL
1 Tbsp.	tarragon wine vinegar	15 mL
2 tsp.	minced fresh garlic	10 mL
2 Tbsp.	anchovy paste	30 mL
1/2 tsp.	dry mustard	3 mL
	Salt and white pepper, to taste	
	Iceberg lettuce	

Combine all ingredients except the lettuce in a food processor. Process until very smooth. Keep in the fridge to use as needed for tossing iceberg lettuce for salads. Also works well as a dip or tossed with hot new potatoes.

MAKES: 2 1/4 c. (560 mL) (Keeps in the refrigerator up to 10 days.)

Serving suggestion: Toss with iceberg lettuce pieces and serve with flatbreads or focaccia as a prelude to almost any meal.

Wine suggestion: Savory, fruity white: '97 Sumac Ridge Sauvignon Blanc, Okanagan, Canada $

NOTE: Green Goddess dressing can be used on any salad greens but the old-fashioned "crunch" of iceberg lettuce is the traditional choice for this dressing.

PRAWNS ON LETTUCE WITH AVOCADO CREAM

This recipe has been adapted from one served at The Oyster Bar on Chuckanut Drive, near Bellingham, Washington. It also works well with fresh crab alone.

16	large raw tiger prawns	16
4	large cooked crab claws	4
Dressing		
2	ripe avocados, peeled, sliced	2
2/3 c.	sour cream	150 mL
1/4 c.	mayonnaise	60 mL
1 Tbsp.	minced fresh tarragon	15 mL
2 Tbsp.	fresh lemon juice	30 mL
	Grated peel of 1 lemon	
1 1/4 tsp.	salt	7 mL
1/4 tsp.	ground white pepper	2 mL
3/4 tsp.	Tabasco	4 mL
	Butter lettuce	
1	large ripe tomato, seeded, diced	1
	Fresh tarragon sprigs	

Drop prawns into boiling salted water in a large saucepan for only about 3-4 minutes. When pink, remove; let stand in ice water while preparing the dressing. Clean crab claws and remove any shell fragments. Combine following 9 dressing ingredients in a food processor or bowl with a hand-held blender. Process until totally smooth. Prepare stem glasses or small cold plates with cups of butter lettuce. Devein prawns; arrange 4 prawns on each plate and one crab claw. Dollop desired amount of avocado cream over and around. Top with diced tomato and additional tarragon. Any unused avocado dressing will keep, tightly covered, one day in the refrigerator.

MAKES: 4 servings

Serving suggestion: Serve as an appetizer with crusty rolls or bread. (Or double the seafood and use as a main course luncheon.)

Wine suggestion: Toasty, buttery white: '96 Lindemans Padthaway Chardonnay, Australia $

SWEET POTATO TERRINE

2 lb.	sweet potatoes or yams, peeled, quartered	1 kg
1	large ripe banana, peeled, cut in 1" (2.5 cm) chunks	1
3 Tbsp.	soft butter	45 mL
3	large eggs, beaten	3
3/4 c.	packed dark brown sugar	175 mL
1/2 c.	dark corn syrup	125 mL
1/2 c.	2% milk	125 mL
1/2 c.	2% evaporated milk	125 mL
1/2 tsp.	vanilla	3 mL
1/2 tsp.	ground mace	3 mL
1/2 c.	golden raisins (*optional*)	125 mL

Cook sweet potatoes in salted boiling water until soft; drain; transfer to bowl of food processor.

Preheat oven to 350ºF. (180ºC).

Pulse sweet potatoes with banana in processor once or twice (do not purée). Transfer to a large bowl; beat in butter; add eggs; beat well; add remaining ingredients; beat until well blended. Pour mixture into a greased or sprayed 9" (23 cm) square pan or loaf pan.

Bake for 1 1/2 hours. Cool in pan for 15 minutes.

MAKES: 6-8 servings

Serving suggestion: Serve warm scoops as a vegetable accompaniment to roasted ham, turkey, chicken; or room temperature slices with whipped cream as a dessert.

Wine suggestion: Honeyed white: '96 Pierre Sparr Pinot Blanc Reserve, Alsace, France $

In Quebec and Ontario, DUC focuses its efforts on wetland protection, restoration and enhancement along the southern Great Lakes and St. Lawrence River. This is an important breeding area for mallards and black ducks and a significant migration route for many populations of geese and diving ducks. DUC has injected $40 million into 800 Ontario projects and $22 million into 150 Quebec wetland sites. Wetland ecosystems are under great threat in this, Canada's most densely populated industrial heartland.

FINISHING TOUCHES

GRAND MARNIER SOUFFLE

3/4 c.	Grand Marnier (or any orange liqueur)	175 mL
2	envl. unflavoured gelatin	2
8	eggs, separated	8
1 c.	sugar, divided	250 mL
1 c.	fresh orange juice	250 mL
1 c.	whipping cream	250 mL
3 Tbsp.	packed golden sugar	45 mL
	Grated peel of 2 large oranges	
2	large oranges, peeled, segmented	2

Combine liqueur and gelatin in a small bowl; let soften while you proceed with the recipe. Place egg yolks and 1/2 c. (125 mL) sugar in a medium saucepan. Use an electric mixer to beat on high speed for at least 4-5 minutes or until yolks are very pale and thick. Gradually beat in orange juice.

Place pan over medium heat; cook, stirring with a wooden spoon or wire whisk until hot and starting to thicken. Gradually stir in softened gelatin and liqueur. Cook and stir until gelatin is dissolved. DO NOT BOIL. When custard is thickened and hot, remove from stove and pour into a bowl. Place a buttered piece of waxed paper on top of the custard to prevent a skin forming. Let stand in front of a fan or in the refrigerator until cold and the consistency of unbeaten egg whites.

In a large bowl, beat egg whites with an electric mixer fitted with wire whisk attachments. Beat until soft peaks form. Gradually start adding remaining 1/2 c. (125 mL) sugar, beating until you have a stiff meringue. In another smaller bowl, beat cream with clean beaters, beating in golden sugar near the end when the cream starts to stiffen. Add cold thickened custard and stiff cream to the meringue bowl. Gently fold together. Spoon into dessert glasses, single serving soufflé dishes (with a collar of foil around the top to show the dessert above the dish rim - see photo) or into a large soufflé dish. Refrigerate at least 3-4 hours until firm.

MAKES: 8-10 servings

Serving suggestion: Serve with extra whipped cream on top and orange peel and segments as decoration (see photo).

Wine suggestion: Luscious dessert wine: '96 Gehringer Riesling Icewine, Okanagan Valley, Canada $$$

CHOCOLATE HAZELNUT MOUSSE CAKE

Brownie base

3/4 c.	hazelnuts (filberts)	175 mL
4	squares semi-sweet chocolate	4
1/4 c.	unsalted butter	60 mL
1/4 c.	Nutella spread *	60 mL
1 Tbsp.	Frangelico liqueur	15 mL
1/4 c.	flour	60 mL
1/4 tsp.	baking powder	2 mL
1/4 c.	sugar	60 mL
1	egg	1

Mousse

5	squares semi-sweet chocolate	5
3/4 c.	unsalted butter, very soft	175 mL
3	eggs, separated	3
2 Tbsp.	Frangelico liqueur	30 mL
1/2 c.	sugar	125 mL

Sauce

1 c.	sour cream	250 mL
1/4 c.	packed golden sugar	60 mL

Thick canned chocolate syrup can be substituted for the Nutella.

Preheat oven to 350ºF. (180ºC). Place nuts on a baking sheet; bake about 7-8 minutes or until toasted. Leave oven on. Place nuts on counter in a clean tea towel; rub hard to remove dark skins. Place nuts in a mini-chop and grind (or chop by hand). Spray or lightly grease a 9" (23 cm) springform pan.

To make the brownie base: place chocolate squares, butter, Nutella and Frangelico in a bowl over a medium saucepan of simmering water. Stir occasionally until completely melted and well combined. Remove from heat. Sift together flour and baking powder onto a piece of waxed paper. Stir in the ground nuts. Using an electric mixer, beat the sugar and egg into the chocolate mixture. Stir in dry ingredients. Pour batter into prepared springform pan. Bake about 7-8 minutes or until a toothpick inserted in the centre comes out clean. Let cool completely on a rack.

To make the mousse: place squares of chocolate in a bowl over a medium saucepan of simmering water to melt. In another larger bowl, beat the butter with an electric mixer until very fluffy and pale in colour. Beat in the egg yolks, melted chocolate and Frangelico. Using a whip attachment on the electric mixer, make the egg whites into a hot meringue by placing whites in a bowl over the simmering water in the saucepan. Beat until very frothy - about halfway to totally beaten. Start to gradually add sugar as you beat. Beat for at least 4-5 minutes or until the meringue is VERY stiff (so that you can cut it with a knife). Make sure that the bowl is not touching the simmering water otherwise the meringue will cook on the bottom of the bowl while you are beating. When the meringue is finished, fold together with the chocolate mixture, not leaving very much meringue showing. Pour onto the cooled crust. Cover tightly with plastic wrap and refrigerate at least 5 hours or overnight. *Let mousse cake stand at room temperature 1/2 hour before serving.* Mix together the sour cream and golden sugar when ready to serve. Cut the mousse cake into wedges and pass the sour cream sauce.

MAKES: 8-10 servings

Serving suggestion: Especially nice with fresh berries in season.

Wine suggestion: Dessert wine: '90 K.W.V. Noble Late Harvest Botrytis affected, South Africa $

Since 1938, Ducks Unlimited Canada has been very active in the conservation, restoration and enhancement of wetland habitat. Although the focus of these efforts has been on waterfowl, the incredible productivity of wetlands and the importance of wetlands for at least part of the life cycle of so many wildlife species has meant that hundreds of species have benefited from the program. DUC projects for waterfowl and wetlands contribute much to the important preservation of Canadian ecological diversity.

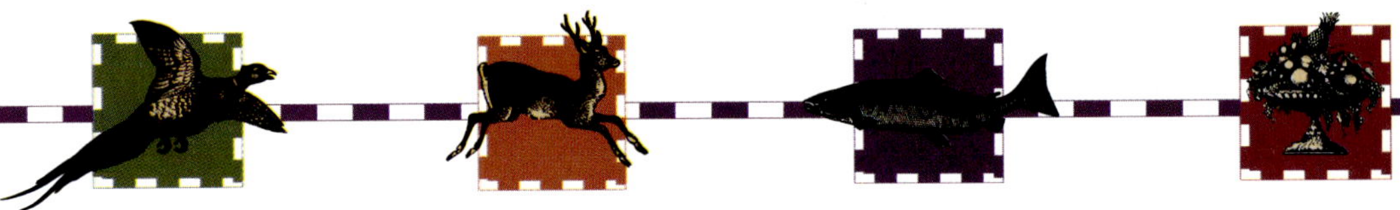

RECIPE INDEX

WINE GUIDE

$ (Inexpensive - under $15 Cdn.) $$ (Moderate - $15 - $20 Cdn.) $$$ (Special Occasion- over $30 Cdn.)

ADVENTURE IN COOKING

Editor and Publisher.. Jan Peskett
Text ....Lyndon Grove
Location Photography .... John Sherlock Studio,
Gunter Marx Photography
Food Photography .... John Sherlock Studio
Recipes ....Ruth Phalen, Jan Peskett,
Jane Thompson, Diane Worthington

Wine Editor.......................................Memory Walsh
Prop Stylist .... Maureen Willick
Editorial Assistant ....Brenda Viney
Design ....Outline Graphic Design Inc.
Production ....LithoTech Canada Ltd.
Printing ....Transcontinental Printing Inc.
Inspiration ....Ducks Unlimited Canada